Compass Points: Creating Meaningful Dialogue

Compass Points: Creating Meaningful Dialogue

Suzanne Ruthven

**COMPASS
BOOKS**

Winchester, UK
Washington, USA

First published by Compass Books, 2014
Compass Books is an imprint of John Hunt Publishing Ltd., Laurel House, Station Approach,
Alresford, Hants, SO24 9JH, UK
office1@jhpbooks.net
www.johnhuntpublishing.com
www.compass-books.net

For distributor details and how to order please visit the 'Ordering' section on our website.

ISBN: 978 1 78279 530 8

A CIP catalogue record for this book is available from the British Library.

Design: Lee Nash

Printed and bound by CPI Group (UK) Ltd, Croydon, CR0 4YY

We operate a distinctive and ethical publishing philosophy in all
areas of our business, from our global network of authors to
production and worldwide distribution.

CONTENTS

Introduction

Poor dialogue is one of the main reasons for a publisher's reader glazing over when reading a first-time novel, where the author has seen fit to include every superfluous utterance of every-day speech. The purpose of dialogue is to move the story along and to give added dimension to the characters through what they say, and often think. *Creating Meaningful Dialogue* helps to get rid of the dross from your typescript and retain the gold in the story. Try to incorporate the exercises given at the end of each chapter into your own writing where appropriate and see how it improves the flow of the dialogue by making the characters come alive. With added input from publishers and publisher's readers, this book is invaluable for all would-be novelists and fiction writers.

Chapter One

Speech Therapy

"Damn!" said the Duchess – is probably one of the most famous opening snatches of dialogue in contemporary literature and yet no one seems to know where it originally came from. A Google entry suggests Agatha Christie but I've yet to locate it in my complete collection of Dame Agatha's creations. Regardless of its provenance, however, this opening line is arresting, *or was in its day*. "Damn" was still a gentleman's oath during mid-war years and rarely uttered in female company never mind attributing it to a lady of such high social standing. So, an opening line such as '"Damn," said the Duchess' was written to shock, to intrigue, to grab the readers' attention – which it certainly did.

Simon Raven used a similar shock tactic some 75-years later with the opening for *Islands of Sorrow*: "Last night," said Adam Ogilvie, "I dreamt I had two pricks." "Where was the second one?" I enquired. This conversation was taking place between two former soldiers and no longer has the power to shock but still managed to intrigue and grab the reader's attention, especially as it was written by literature's premier *enfant terrible* of the time. Here dialogue provides that essential 'hook' that writing tutors talk about for setting the opening of the novel; without that captivating hook the novel flounders before it even gets off the first page. A snappy one-liner uttered by the novel's principal character still has the power to grip the imagination and get the reader gasping for more lines of captivating dialogue.

The *Chambers Concise Dictionary's* definition of 'dialogue' is 'conversation between two or more people, especially of a formal or imaginary nature; the lines spoken by characters in plays, films, novels, etc; an exchange of views in the hope of ultimately reaching agreement'. Sounds quite easy and straightforward? On the contrary. Good dialogue is extremely difficult to write and taking into account that – by rule of thumb – a novel should consist of 50-60 per cent dialogue, we begin to realise just how important it is to understand the mechanics of it if we are going to produce a saleable novel.

Publishers from one John Hunt Publishing imprint often act as readers for the other imprints, and are asked to prepare readers' reports for a wide variety of novels aimed at an even wider variety of genres. And the most common fault that throws a spanner in the works in the readability stakes is the poor use of dialogue – either pages of meaningless rambling, or hardly any dialogue at all. In fact, as Compass Books author Susan Palmquist so rightly observes in *How To Write A Romance Novel*, dialogue can make or break a story.

Dialogue has several roles to play in novel writing but these tricks should be used in tandem with the narrative, not as a replacement. For example it can be used to:

- move the plot along
- reveal character and personality
- impart information
- condense history or background
- introduce drama
- deliberately mislead
- cause confusion
- inject humour

Move the plot along

If we're writing a family saga we will follow our characters literally from the cradle to the grave but in the majority of novels, we begin with the current day's action – which means there are large gaps to be filled in along the way. Background detail can be added quickly by characters who were around at the time recounting their memories of what happened under a variety of different circumstances pertaining to the plot. A good example is the way the dialogue with researchers, librarians or archivists is included in the television programme *Who Do You Think You Are?* – there is an economy of language in the programme editing that moves the story along to fit the one hour slot while still conveying the important points of the story. Elderly relatives and family friends are useful for this particular technique and are characters that can be wheeled in purely for this purpose – and wheeled out again.

In Douglas Kennedy's novel *The Woman in the Fifth*, the background information for the story was supplied by a friend of the main character keeping him informed by e-mail of what was happening on the other side of the world – the emails counting as dialogue. Using this device means that information can be included at the right time in the narrative without any lengthy preliminary build-up; it can also be used without the need for a character having a valid reason for being in a particular location in order to receive the information. Or finding old letters, or diaries – such as those used by Harlan Coben in *Play Dead*, where the descendants discover a dire family secret that pulls all the strands of the mystery together as they discuss it between themselves.

Reveal character and personality

The personality, and often character, of a person can be portrayed in the way they speak. We can also learn a lot from well-written television where snappy lines have been written around often-conflicting characters. Study the popular series *New Tricks*, for instance and the diverse characters who deliver the dialogue: the abrasive and ambitious female lead, Sandra; Jack, the grieving widower and former murder squad detective; lecherous Gerry and the compulsive-obsessive alcoholic Brian. As *The Guardian's* reviewer wrote: "Fresh, original and funny ...

for a masterclass in effortless character acting look no further." The sharp, witty dialogue is set against a brutal backdrop of murder but the scriptwriting allows each character to stamp their own mark on each episode through the medium of good dialogue.

Television drama at its best is often the best way to study how to write dialogue since scriptwriting has to make every line count by being both pertinent to the story *and* the character delivering the lines. We watch the finished *visual* product but in the creative stages, the scriptwriter is 'seeing' the characters speaking the lines in his mind's eye – just as the novelist is doing when putting words into their characters' mouths. Where the story is character-led the dialogue focuses on building the main character(s); where the story is plot-led the drama doesn't have time for extraneous dialogue and the mood is often set by the banter between colleagues or friends during the action. Crime thriller writers Jonathan Kellerman, Harlan Coben and Michael Connelly are excellent examples of this technique.

Impart information

Sometimes it's necessary to impart technical or background information to the reader and rather than using pages of research notes to pad out the story, one character can give the information to another in a variety of different scenarios. Usually this type of information is an important part of the story and needs to be covered in some depth within the narrative – but often over a period of time. In *Riptide* by Lincoln Preston, and possibly the best treasure hunt adventure since *Treasure Island*, the author uses pages of the kidnapped architect's coded journal to add to the sense of 17th-century drama coupled with 21st-century technology, while the ensuing dialogue between the members of the team explains things in lay-terms to the reader.

The Wild Horseman is set during the first two weeks of WWII following Dunkirk, and the dialogue is taken from actual events and happenings that were reported on a weekly basis by *The War Illustrated*, the British propaganda newspaper of the time. The whole novel revolves around two characters whose mission is to bring two valuable racehorses back to England before they can be requisitioned by the advancing German army. The text is mainly dialogue as the older man tries to teach a naive 16-year old girl how to live off the land and survive the perils they encounter. At the start, dialogue is formal as it would have been between a 1930s landowner and a stable-girl, but as the adventure unfolds and the camaraderie grows, the conversation develops into something much more relaxed and familiar.

By contrast *Polar Shift* by Clive Cussler tries to avert a catastrophic event that will cause earthquakes, lava eruptions, tsunamis and giant whirlpools in what is best described as a science fiction adventure. The dialogue between the scientists leaves no room for lay-person's terminology so any problematic theories are dealt with by another member of the team asking questions to clarify the situation, especially when the subject under discussion isn't his particular discipline and he needs an explanation.

Condense history or background

Even contemporary novels require a certain amount of 'history' or background to give the characters a setting in which to act. A conversation between two people is an effective way of providing this information where a long screed of detail would throw the narrative out of kilter. For example:

"You know Simon's background, of course. Father was a Billingsgate porter who married a coloured dancer," remarked Betty.

"No, I didn't know, but that must account for those sultry good looks," replied Babs.

"Personally, I find him rather oily," came the response.

You old cat, thought Babs, *you didn't think like that at Veronica's 40th when you tried to get him into your bedroom.*

Fuller details of Simon's parentage can be dealt with in depth where appropriate in the narrative, but for now it's only hinted at during a bout of gossip to give the reader a tang of mystery. The question of how Simon improved himself socially is what would encourage the reader to read on.

Introduce drama

All novels contain an element of drama – a series of exciting, tense, tragic events that bring out the vices and virtues of the characters. Even the most genteel romance needs to have tension to give substance to a story and this is often created by one character alluding to some mysterious happening that subsequently erupts into a full-scale drama. Using dialogue to create drama can be an overheard conversation, or a repeated exchange that is quoted out of context – deliberately or otherwise. The introduction of drama is all a matter of timing and a technique that can often be used to kick-start a flagging story-line: "Did you know that your mother had an affair with the Aga Khan?" cousin Millie asked a little too casually – is the kind of line that would produce a reaction under any circumstances.

Perhaps the ace of writers of this technique is non-fiction writer Richard Preston (and brother of fiction author Douglas Preston), a science writer who tells his factual stories in the style of a novel. *The Hot Zone* and *First Light* are light years away from each other in subject matter but by using the technique of writing dialogue for the real people featured in the text, there is a very human interest angle injected into these dramatic true stories.

Deliberately mislead

Misunderstanding is the other essential element of the novel because without the misunderstandings between the principal characters the story has no momentum. This is, of course, the quintessential verbal 'red herring' so important to the thriller writer and particularly Agatha Christie who was so adept at misleading her readers into suspecting completely the wrong person until the dénouement tidies up all the loose ends.

In my horror novel, *Whittlewood*, I used an interview with a journalist to include an extract from a book to side-step a pertinent question about the personal beliefs of the speaker and to provide some important background information about the character:

"The few journalists I have talked to, seem to prefer ideas in set out paragraphs, in words they can spell. For the benefit of your readership I'll quote you a passage by William James, which is far more eloquent than I could ever be. Bearing in mind he made his observations in 1890, very few original ideas have actually been added since." She indicated with her hand that she wished him to use his small tape recorder and removing a book from the shelf, began to read.

"The phenomena are there, lying broadcast over the surface of history. No matter where you open its pages, you find things recorded under the name of divinations, inspirations, demoniacal possessions, apparitions, traces, ecstasies, miraculous healings, productions of disease and occult powers, possessed by peculiar individuals over persons and things in their neighbourhood.

"We suppose that mediumship originated in Rochester and animal magnetism with Mesmer but one look behind the pages of official history, in personal memoirs, legal documents, popular narratives and books of anecdote, and you will find that there never was a time when these things were not reported just as abundantly as now ... a public no less large keeps and transmits from generation

to generation the traditions and practices of the occult."

There was a brief silence in the room as she replaced the book.

"Do you want me to quote James?"

"As you wish but I doubt if either you or I could explain any better where my ideas come from. I don't go in for gore, my style is to create a story around historical phenomena that hopefully encourages people to consider the paranormal as something perfectly natural."

"Natural?"

"Just because there is no *immediate* explanation on tap, it doesn't mean that it's unnatural or that a solution doesn't exist."

This short extract serves a triple purpose in that it shifts the onus of defining the main character's belief onto another author, and imparts information pertinent to the story – while indicating that the character has little time or trust when it comes to journalists.

The conversation between the US President and the television anchor-woman in the opening chapters of Edwin Corley's *Sargasso* prevents a potentially damaging broadcast from going out as the two characters bandy words in an almost flirtatious manner. By the time the woman realises that the compliments and small talk are serving a different purpose, the FBI have moved in and everyone is being detained – with the minimum amount of fuss and news coverage! It is not until the dialogue at the end of the novel that the President's motives are made clear but up until then he's been considered the bad guy.

Cause confusion

Causing confusion may not be a deliberate action but a genuine 'slip of the tongue' whereby wrong information is imparted by the speaker to another, or is overheard by a third party. This is a useful device for introducing misunderstandings, red herrings, misinterpretation and gossip to create the essential sub-plot, without which any novel is doomed to fail. For example, a 'daily' woman can be overheard in the Post Office saying that she'd seen Mrs Brown's new lover in the conservatory. Gossip spreads around the village like wildfire before it is finally revealed that the poor woman has had new a *louvre* blind fitted to keep out the sun!

Inject humour

Humour is a difficult thing to use successfully although the most effective way to use it in a novel is to have first-class one-liners spoken by the characters in response to another's comment, or to lighten a situation. Black humour is appropriate in serious novels involving the emergency services and military because that's how personnel cope with grim situations in real life situations. Douglas Preston can create heart-stopping moments of high drama or disperse them with just a casual throw-away line as when one of his team in *The Hot Zone* is about to go into a deadly virus-infected area in a biological suit: He contemplated me with an amused look and said, "If you were four inches long and suddenly appeared on my floor, I would be forced to do something drastic."

New Tricks gets away with non-PC humour because the characters are all post-retirement age detectives and the humour reflects attitudes in policing *as it was in their time*, despite the disapproval of their female 'guvner'. The important thing is not to let the conversation develop into a stand-up comedy routine, otherwise it loses impact when the two speakers are trying to outdo each other in the witty stakes. Use humour sparingly for the best effect – such as: "And this from the woman who considers *The Duchess of Malfi* light entertainment" in response to a comment that a colleague should learn to lighten up a bit.

The Book of Tells by Peter Collett explains that when we're talking to people, we tend to focus on *what* they say, rather than the way they say it, or the precise expressions they use, and we should be aware of this when constructing dialogue. For example:

Pronouns: People who frequently use the word 'I' tend to be concerned with themselves and can be used to imply arrogance or selfishness. Those who prefer to use 'we' are often trying to avoid making any reference of themselves as individuals, but it can also be used to misleadingly imply that someone else is in agreement with them. "We think you could have got better results, don't we Mum?"

Attractors: People who show a preference to 'name-dropping', 'place-dropping' or 'experience-dropping'. Of the three, name-dropping is the most effective means of trying to increase social status by implying a more intimate relationship with a celebrity than is true. "As I said to Ken only the other day, the play's the thing." "Where are you staying for Henley?" "Hearing Dame Kiri sing the Marschallin was such a wonderful experience." The listener is supposed to know exactly to what and whom the speaker is referring, or has to display their ignorance by asking.

Deflectors: People who are shy or want to avoid the attention of others often resort to what are known as 'linguistic deflectors'. Deliberately asking other people questions about themselves, or steering the conversation towards topics closer to the other person's interest. This automatically shifts the spotlight away from themselves and reduces the chances that they will have to reveal something of a personal nature. "What a beautiful necklace Mrs Worthington, is it a family piece?"

Contrastors: The injection of words like 'but', 'however' and 'nevertheless' are used by people who like to point out that things aren't always what they seem and who want to put forward another point of view. "I think you have a very valid point, Mike – however ...."

Softeners: People often say things that are designed to soften the impact of what they are going to say next. As a prelude to criticism or as a device to be rude while denying that is their intention "I hope you don't mind me saying, Audrey ..."

Hedges: Everyday speech is full of 'hedges' – expressions such as 'well', 'sort of', 'kind of', 'like' and 'you know' – but they don't work in written dialogue. The odd sprinkling here and here is permissible but a page full of "errs", "umms" and "dunnos" is extremely tedious in a novel even if they are part of normal, every-day speech patterns.

One-worders: One worders, such as "Oh dear", "Okay", "Really?" or "Fine" can speak volumes when placed strategically in a conversation.

It should have become evident by now that the insertion of dialogue into a story is a highly important part of the construction of any type of fiction. For the first draft it can be added "as it is spoken" but by the final draft this should have been honed like a fine sword with a fine cutting edge and sharp delivery. Try these two exercises:

Exercise 1:
We all know the importance of impact first-liners for a story but they also need to serve the purpose of pulling the reader into the narrative. Try writing your own opening first lines of dialogue that could be used for a novel or short story. For example: "I wouldn't worry about who moved your pen, Mr President. There's a nuclear missile heading straight for the Oval Office,

even as we speak."

This short piece of dialogue sets the scene and tells us everything we need to know at the start of a story: time (modern day), place (Oval Office, Washington, USA), character (President – pernickety: speaker – Mr Cool) and on-going drama (impending missile attack).

Get into the habit of recognising useful snippets of dialogue and for goodness sake write them down, we think we'll remember them but we don't!

Exercise 2:
In real-time speech we have the benefit of inflection and nuance to convey exactly what the speaker intends; with written dialogue things aren't so cut and dried. For example: *"I have never used cheap perfume. You must be confusing me with someone else."*

As it stands, this statement could be read as defensive, reflective, a put-down, a question, or an accusation. Let's start with a defensive tone...

"I have never used cheap perfume. You must be confusing me with someone else," cried Barbara thrusting away the cloying scented handkerchief with its tell-tale initial 'B' soaked in blood. Or reflective...

"I have never used cheap perfume. You must be confusing me with someone else," murmured Alison aloud, wondering who could be the owner of the sickly-sweet scent. Or as a put-down...

"I have never used cheap perfume. You must be confusing me with someone else," retorted Fiona, dismissing the embarrassed young man with a toss of her head. Or a question...

"I have never used cheap perfume. You must be confusing me with someone else?" smiled Lady Allan handing the familiar glove back to the Inspector, but not wanting to terminate the interview without knowing how he'd come by it. Or an accusation...

"I have never used cheap perfume. You must be confusing me with someone else," snapped Jayne, holding the offending shirt under her husband's nose.

This exercise demonstrates the importance of reading dialogue aloud. Try reading aloud all the lines above in turn with the appropriate inflection and imagine following the 'stage directions' for each one so that you can hear the difference.

Chapter Two

Historical Discourse

The greatest writers of historical dialogue are, of course, Shakespeare and of a later period, Balzac – but neither would receive much acclaim in today's publishing world – simply because no one speaks like that any more ... more's the pity. Wouldn't it be much nicer to greet our partner on his return home with the words: "How fares my lord?" rather than "Had a good day, dear?" or "God grant thee good speed," instead of: "See yer ..." but unfortunately, like everything else in life, dialogue alters drastically from generation to generation.

The Daily Telegraph recently featured a new reference book, *Shakespeare's Words*, co-authored by professor of linguistics, David Crystal and his actor son Ben that reveals our modern lack of understanding of Shakespeare is due to incorrect pronunciation. The key, they believe is understanding the original, which was a mixture of contemporary accents used in the early 17th-century and have produced a guide that includes a host of puns, jokes and rhymes that could be useful to the writer to create the atmosphere of the period. For example: "In ACT II of *As You Like It*, Jacques talks about a joke he heard, apparently about time: *'From hour to hour, we ripe and ripe, from hour to hour we rot and rot, and thereby hangs a tale.'* Hour would be pronounced the same as 'whore', turning it into a bawdy joke."

The Penguin Dictionary of Historical Slang also provides another insight into the "rich idiom of English life through the ages, bringing back to mind the vigour of Elizabethan phrase, the ribald language of dockside and pub, the richer coinage of mess-deck and barrack, the euphemisms and witticisms of the Victorian drawing-room, and the irrepressible wit of errand boys and costermongers".

For the historical novelist, reference books such as these are invaluable since they offer snatches of speech, colloquialisms, and turns of phrase that we need to convey to the reader a sense of time and place in a language they can easily understand. *The Book of Etiquette* by Laura, Lady Troubridge, for example, reveals what was considered socially correct at the time of going to press. This title was first published in 1926; updated in 1958, with a sixth edition published in 1976 but as the author observes in her Foreword:

> "Etiquette may be defined as the technique of the art of social life. For various and good reasons certain traditions have been handed down, just as they are in any other art, science, or department of life, and only very thoughtless persons could consider unworthy to notice that set of rules which guides us in our social relations to each other."

If we wish to write period fiction then we need to know how people of that particular time related to each other, not just to those of their own station but people of higher or inferior rank. An even earlier edition of Ward Locks's *Etiquette For Gentlemen* advises on the manners and behaviour required for all social occasions during the Edwardian period with gems such as this one for the hunting field: "A man may forgive you for breaking his daughter's heart, but never for breaking his hunter's neck!" Lines like this can be re-used in dialogue to add an authentic feel to the conversation.

Books of 'manners' have been around for a long time and using authentic background information from them can add depth to the narrative, as well as giving rise to some captivating and amusing dialogue. The first recorded version appears to have been *The Maxims of Ptahhotep* written by an Old Kingdom vizier of that name from fifth-Dynasty Egypt. All literate civilizations, including ancient Greece and Rome, developed rules for proper social conduct and Gore Vidal put this dialogue to good use in *Julian*, his historical novel about the last pagan Emperor of Rome.

To find out what are the most common faults in the dialogue in historical novels, we turn to Autumn Barlow, publisher of Top Hat Books, specialising in all types of historical fiction from the ancient world to WWII. What would her advice be to budding historical novelists?

"We ought to remember that no dialogue is ever written exactly as people speak. Just take a look at a transcript of actual speech – it's all ums, ahs, and vague noises. Written dialogue in a novel is a careful construct, and it's a tricky balance to convey a sense of naturalism without ending up like a court report. So, if we accept the 'natural' dialogue in books is actually 'artificial' then why do historical novelists insist on stilted phrases, outdated vocabulary and endless, endless sentences? I fear that they are relying too heavily on 'thee' and 'thou' to create a sense of history when, in fact, that period feeling ought to be coming from much more subtle clues. Attitudes, scene-setting, even a character's name will give a book a historical setting that no amount of 'prithee good sir, I bid you tidings of the King' can do. Remember what your book is *for*. To entertain, educate, to delight, to challenge – all these things are good but you must get the reader on your side, and identifying with the characters, and you are going to make that so much harder if the characters talk like a 1940s Errol Flynn epic.

"I also read a lot of otherwise good books where the characters speak as if they are mimicking the characters in a Jane Austen book. Just because the characters in *Emma* spoke in a particular way, you cannot assume that everyone living at that time also spoke that way – I refer you back to my earlier point – written dialogue is *not* representative of real speech, and never has been. Obviously you need to avoid modern slang, but there is no need to avoid contractions (unless the character warrants it) and there's no need to have them using long words and tortuous sentences (again, unless it is needed by the personality of the character). I am sure that eighth-century peasants said "Oi! Put that down!" to their kids as much as we do."

We also have to take into account when writing historical novels, that there are often conflicting cultures to be taken into account that can enrich a story, but also leave the modern reader feeling cheated if they are glossed over, or the author fails to address them in a satisfactory manner. And yet there are times when common interest transcends the language/cultural barrier – a device I used several times for *The Wild Horseman* because the entire story focussed on just two people, with lots of carefully choreographed 'walk-on' parts – such as the common universal bond between horsey people. Even Sherlock Holmes commented on this: "There is a wonderful sympathy and freemasonry among horsey men. Be one of them, and you will know all there is to know."

For example: during an encounter with a German paratrooper this 'freemasonry' averts what could have been a nasty moment and demonstrates how this technique can be used to transcend international barriers and politics:

The two men were still locked in eye contact when there was suddenly a visual shift in the German's expression. He frowned, as if trying to recall a detail to mind. "I know you," he said finally.

Richard shook his head. "I don't think so."

"Yes! We *have* met before." The automatic was lowered slightly and for the first time he looked at the horses with a different eye as recognition dawned. "You have been to Schlenderhahn ... *Herr* Hunter ... is it not?"

He? was close enough for Richard to be able to believe that

he might have met this young German before, but he could not honestly remember. "You worked at Schlenderhahn?" he asked, desperately trying to recall mental pictures of the faces of the grooms and riders from the famous German stud.

By this time the German was so relieved to have found a friendly face that he struggled to put the pistol back in his pocket. "*Ya!* For *Herr* Oppenheim. You rode out with us several times."

"I remember riding out," said Richard slowly, picturing the early morning gallops but still unable to place the soldier.

"You do not remember me?"

"Sorry, no. What's your name?" he asked, playing for time. The pistol had disappeared but he was not about to relax his guard.

"Klaus von Nehring, *Herr* Hunter. It does not matter that you do not remember me, but it is fortunate that I remember you, no?"

Richard smiled but remained non-committal. "So it would seem. What do you propose to do now?"

For the first time, the German appeared tired and sad, his expression old beyond his years. "You must go, *Herr* Hunter," he said, suddenly serious and insistent. "I will find another way to help my companion. His leg is broken and your horses would have been ideal ... but we are not enemies you and I. It would not be right." Von Nehring stepped to the side and held out his hand. "When the war is over, we will meet at your Cheltenham and we will drink together."

Richard took his hand. "I'll look forward to that."

The 'horsey' dialogue was provided by a friend who had himself 'ridden under rules' as a professional jockey and was a racehorse trainer, to give authenticity to the conversation. For example during this early extract:

By now, the bread was hard and the cheese sweaty but

stretched out on the sunlit bank, it was easy to forget that they were fleeing from a war zone. Deep in the quiet of the French countryside, the sounds of distant fighting was almost inaudible and for all they knew, the opposing armies could have settled their differences and called it a day.

"Can we stop for food tomorrow and find out what's going on?" she asked.

"That's what I was thinking. It's pointless skulking about like this if the war is over. Although that's probably wishful thinking on my part," Richard added, closing his eyes against the sun's glare as he leant his head back against the saddle. "Not only that, the horses are going to need some hard corn, because without it they'll soon drop away on just grass and be unfit for any excessive riding *should* it become necessary."

"You mean should we have to make a run for it?"

"Something like that," he murmured drowsily.

"But why haven't we seen anyone?" persisted Jenny.

"I've no idea but there's sure to be a good reason. It's Sunday and they'll all be in church, praying like mad for deliverance."

"Mr Todhunter!"

Richard opened one eye. "I don't believe praying got you anywhere unless you're willing to back it up with a bit of action for your own part. We could have prayed from now until Doomsday but nothing would have got us out of the Leroux's place except our own endeavours."

In just this short piece the reader understands the importance of keeping the horses well-fed – that grass in insufficient for the job in hand; and it reveals something about the main character – that he is resilient and resourceful. It also shows the formality that exists between the pair at the beginning of their adventure.

Another genre that falls under the historical banner is the Western. Although not as popular as in the days of Zane Grey's classic *Riders of the Purple Sage,* when westerns offered an idealised, mythical view of the Old West, they still have a keen following, providing the perspective is brought up to date and not left back in the early 1950s. And the main difference between then and now is the way dialogue is used to tell the story. In *How To Write A Western in 30 Days,* Nik Morton suggests that dialogue should convey the period, the person's profession and background, and the character with the use of appropriate vocabulary; but, as he also points out, "dialogue isn't always in speech – but in body language" to suggest mood or emotion in a scene.

In the American 'Wild West', however, there is also another example of a conflicting culture to be taken into account – that of the Native Americans. In *Everyday Life Among The American Indians* Candy Moulton provides a guide for writers, students and historians because, as she so rightly points out: "Nothing in the chronicle of American history has been more riddled with stereotypes and falsehoods than the lives of the American Indians and the vital role they played in our nation's past." And dialogue was a complex matter:

"Across North America Indians spoke one of six language types. Three were major – the Algonquian, Athapascan (or Athabaskan) and Siouian – and these formed the basis of language for many tribes (though each tribe had variations). ... As a result of these language differences ... neighbouring tribes couldn't necessarily communicate easily with each other, not even if they were technically blood relatives. People of the Plains developed a universal sign language that involved hand motions to represent words and phrases."

So if your US Army scout is going to perform some masterful feat of negotiation, you would be well advised to give him the right pedigree to be able to pull it off. For the western story-teller it might be an idea to obtain a copy of W F Clarke's *The Indian Sign Language* – originally written for army use in 1882 and re-published by the University of Nebraska Press in 1982.

Oaths are authentic devices used to liven up dialogue since they are common-place speech in historical novels from any period. The dictionary definition being: 'an expression used lightly irreverently, exclamatorily, decoratively or in imprecation'. Oaths and slang had their fashionable periods and would probably have been picked up by the different social classes depending on their dealings with the class below themselves. They add colour to dialogue but we should avoid the use of slang without giving an explanation. For example:

"By the piper that played before Moses" is an asseveration (c.1858) used lightly or irreverently in place of a solemn declaration. It is classed as a low colloquialism that might have been used by males of the lower and middle classes. "By the piper that played before Moses, I swear I'll marry you tomorrow." And we know he won't!

"A man is said to' stand Moses' when he has another man's bastard child fathered upon him, and he is obliged by the parish to maintain it." [*Penguin Dictionary of Historical Slang*] Dating from c1790 in common speech this type of saying can easily be worked into a conversation with the first speaker using the phrase and a second giving the explanation:

"I'll be damned if I'll stand Moses to Amos's bastard," said Dick, slurring his speech.

"Ay, it's no laughing matter to have another man's child foisted upon him and being obliged by the parish to pay for it!" agreed Thomas.

A c1630 saying that *"You shall have moonshine in the mustard pot for it"* can be reworked as: "And what have I got to show for it?"

asked Nell, "Moonshine in a mustard pot! Nothing!"

"To roast a stone" means to waste time and energy and dates from c1520-1620 and could be used as: "I'd just as likely roast a stone, as waste time looking for work in these parts."

As Autumn Barlow points out, written dialogue is *not* representative of real speech, and never has been, but we can research our period closely and still add some delightful authentic gems to lighten the conversation – and pass on a little of our new-found knowledge. Try these two exercises:

Exercise 1:
Using genuine research material such as *The Ration Book Diet WWII* by Mike Brown, Carol Harris and CJ Jackson (Sutton), *Food & Feast in Medieval England* by Peter Hammon (Sutton), *Food in the Ancient World* by John M Wilkins and Shaun Hill (Blackwell) or *An Ancient Egyptian Herbal* by Lise Manniche (BMP), create period dialogue about the food those people would have been eating. Obtain books on food, etiquette, etc., relating to your novel's period and use the information to add depth to your writing.

By using dialogue to describe the food of the day, we can add depth to our novel without venturing into the realms of lengthy narrative and descriptive passages, while giving our characters something to talk about!

Exercise 2:
The use of historical slang in dialogue helps to set the tone for time and place but it is essential that our 'sayings' fit the correct era to which they belong. Much of what we quote in fiction is what was known as 'grafter's slang' used by those who worked at fairs and markets such as fortune-tellers and quack doctors. Some of it is 'parley', some Romany, some Yiddish, some

rhyming slang and 'cant' – the language of the underworld. Parley for example includes the 'lingua Franca' a mixture of Italian, French, Greek and Spanish originally used for communication between traders in the Mediterranean and Near East.

In later times some 90% of its words came from c18th-mid-19th actors and mid c19[th]-20th costermongers and showmen. Take for example the term 'Billingsgate' to describe someone who is foul-mouthed. The term can be traced back to 17th century physician and failed wit Edmund Gayton quote from c1654 – "Most bitter Billingsgate rhetoric ..." – but by 1800 it was recognised as standard English usage. Here we could have a character use the c19-20th colloquialism: "She's no better than a Billingsgate fish-fag" to mean a foul-mouthed woman or 'fishwife'. Use *The Penguin Dictionary of Historical Slang* to enrich your character's dialogue.

Remember that slang percolates upwards from the lower classes and that your characters will have to have a reason for coming into contact with its usage and including it in their own vocabulary. Young hell-rakes frequenting taverns, play-houses and brothels would have easy access but to their elders it would have been a foreign language. Have fun using slang but make sure your dating is correct and that an explanation is included in the text.

Chapter Three

Chit-chat and Small Talk

As Peter Collett points out in *The Book of Tells*, the most obvious thing about conversation is that people usually take turns in delivering their lines. Although it is considered unusual for more than one person to be talking at a time, it is an indication that the conversation has temporarily broken down if 'multiple input' continues for any length of time. In popular television programmes, however, it is now normal for three, four or even more people to be talking at the same time – completely ignoring the fact that the human brain cannot register 'talk' and 'listen' at the same time.

> "Psychologists who study conversation have found that people are remarkably skilled at taking turns. They have discovered that the time that elapses between one person completing their turn and the next person starting to talk can be so brief as to be almost non-existent – in some instances it's less than 50 thousandths of a second! These are all 'smooth transitions', because the switch between one speaker and the next is so seamless."

When we're including chit-chat and small talk in a novel it still needs to serve a purpose. Character's reactions to one another can be expressed in the way we introduce them into the conversation and reveal a lot about an individual's personality without resorting to lengthy description. A lengthy monologue, for example, used to explain a situation can be broken up by 'back-channelling' – having the listener giving a series of verbal responses such as "uh-huh", "yeah", "um", "really" accompanied by nods and smiles, which show that the listener is agreeing with the speaker whilst not getting in the way of the narrative.

Autumn Barlow of Top Hat Books comments about the problems she encounters when acting as a publisher's reader for other genres:

"As a reader, I feel tired when I see walls of text with no dialogue. For me, dialogue is the quickest way to get under a character's skin and understand them. I want to connect with the characters I read about. Don't tell me that Susie is a prissy madam with a superiority complex – show me how she speaks to the acne-covered shop girl.

I also feel there is a place for more humour in dialogue. I enjoy contemporary romances, and the ones I like best are where the hero and heroine's dialogue sparkles with wit and interaction. In real life we joke, make puns, engage in word play – so why, in some novels, do the characters merely expound the most turgid and boring things to each other?

Again it's a balance. In real life we don't take it in turns to speak, but in written dialogue there has to be more structure. But I hate to read the sort of dialogue where it almost feels like a bunch of actors taking it in turns to read from a script. I sometimes get the feeling that writers don't read their work out loud. That's a basic part of writing, I think. Read your dialogue out loud! If you stumble to a halt, something needs to change."

From these comments we can see that deep, heavy dialogue isn't always necessary to move things along, chit-chat and small talk in a novel also serves that purpose as a perfect character-revealing device. Gossipy scenarios with two or more characters involved can provide opportunities for revealing all sorts of little quirks and foibles about those taking part in your story. For example:

"It's like living with bloody Eeyore!" grumbled Jayne. "His glass is always half empty, while mine is half full."

This snippet speaks volumes about Jayne and her absent partner and yet this could be a one-liner thrown casually into small talk. Firstly, it shows she has a quirky sense of humour in likening her partner to a gloomy, pessimistic character in a children's book. The comment tells us that they are opposites and suggests that it may be causing problems in their relationship because her irritation is showing through. While Jayne is obviously a positive, upbeat sort of person, her partner is seen as perpetually miserable.

The technique of name-dropping manages to convey more than just a means of impressing other people. In *Name Dropping? A No-Nonsense Guide to the Use of Names in Everyday Language* by Philip Gooden we are treated to an aromatic pot-pourri of names used to characterise something else. The collection shows how expressions derived from people and places can be wide-ranging and even contradictory in their implications. As the author explains:

"Politicians are pleased to be called *Churchillian* ... but which aspect of Churchill are we talking about? Is it his speech-making or inspirational leadership; is it his capacity for drink, or his well-known bouts of depression? Writers are *Dickensian* if they throw a grotesque character or two into the mix, but the expression is just as frequently used to describe a grimy, real-life scene straight out of the 19th century while, paradox-ically, it can also mean 'sentimental' or conjure up the image of a cosy, old-fashioned Christmas."

Nevertheless, the technique of using name-dropping to embellish our dialogue can speak volumes in itself. As Philip Gooden points out, the *way* a name is used is also significant in that by adding 'ite' (*Thatcherite* or *Blairite*) we can turn a compliment into an insult; while using the softer 'esque' or 'ist' or 'ian' can produce a more neutral effect. A nice snobby put-down is illustrated by Gooden's observation that: "Film buffs will talk happily about *Cronenbergian* or *Bunuelesque*, while *Hitchcockian* is much more widely understood." The latter can be used in dialogue to shut someone out, for example:

"What would you say were the outstanding merits of Cronenberg's style over those of Buñuel?"

How many of us (even cinema lovers) could respond to that one if it were thrown into the conversation at a party! And yet if the question were asked at a foreign (or fringe) film festival it would be a perfectly natural conversation piece. In *Charnel House Blues*, I frequently used the term *Byronic* to describe the classic literary vampire, who tells the story in the guise of Polidori's Lord Ruthven.

Although children's fiction doesn't have huge tracts of dialogue like some adult fiction, there are still some important 'rules' to be observed even when keeping it simple. We asked Maria Moloney, publisher of Lodestone and Our Street children's fiction what she thought were the most common mistakes made when writing dialogue for children and young adults. Her response:

"A child speaking in adult voice. Don't bestow words and phrases on child characters that only an adult would use. When writing dialogue you should consider if a child would really say the phrase you are writing. Would they think those things in that way? Would they act that way? Remember, the child is not you, and would not say things the way you would. **Example:** 'The bond between parent and child is strong,' said Lucy.

Better: 'I love my mum, and she loves me,' said Lucy.
Example: 'Do you not care about my well-being?' asked Jack.
Better: 'Don't you care about me?' asked Jack.
If in doubt as to what children like to read these days, visit the local bookshop or library. Visit the section with books that cover the age range you are interested in writing for and then read as many as possible. Do ensure your main characters are a similar age to the age group aimed at. Take note of the level of language used, the structure and length of the book."

While on the subject, we asked her to put on her John Hunt Publishing reader's hat and give her general observations about the use of dialogue in other genres.

Overuse of dialogue tags more often happens in romance novels: This doesn't mean you shouldn't use them at all. But some people go to a lot of trouble to avoid writing a simple "said", when most of the time "said" does just fine. In addition you can "whisper" words but you can't "smile" them, "laugh" "scowl" or "grin" them.

Common variations are he smiled, laughed, grinned, mumbled, pleaded, responded, yelled, mused, whimpered, and sighed – anything but "said" in fact.

Overuse of adverbs: Use sparingly, and only if the words don't speak for themselves, and it's too difficult to get the phrase to do this adequately. Common ones are "she said admiringly", softly, loudly, sarcastically, bravely, timidly, angrily, impatiently, sharply, kindly, anxiously, cheerily, soothingly, quickly, quietly, absentmindedly, bitterly, boastfully, excitedly, dreamily, briskly, bleakly, fiercely, joyfully, knowingly, solemnly, reproachfully, viciously, wisely, woefully and so forth.

A combination of the previous two points: pleaded anxiously, shouted loudly, responded sarcastically, whimpered softly, laughed cheerfully, mumbled quietly and so on.

Example: 'I'd be delighted,' he smiled cheerfully.

Better: He smiled. 'I'd be delighted.'

Example: 'I'm not so sure,' he carefully mused.

Better: Tom scratched his chin. 'I'm not so sure.'

Short story writing is probably the most popular form of creative writing of all and needs to use chit-chat and small talk to its best advantage because the narrative is restricted to a pre-set word count in the magazine (or competition). If your story exceeds the parameters set by the magazine's editor or the competition organiser then it will be rejected, no matter how good the writing. In *How To Write and Sell Great Short Stories*, Linda M James makes some interesting observations about dialogue and how to use it to make every word count!

"Remember also that every word your characters say needs to fit a specific purpose. Simply moving the story forward isn't enough. It must also reveal nuances of their character, reveal a tiny fragment of their back-story, and suggest their relationship to the character they're speaking with."

Linda James also reminds us that although description and dialogue are usually discussed as entirely separate techniques, conveying description through dialogue is a challenge. However, as characters view people, events or situations from differing viewpoints, the kind of dialogue they use tells us a great deal about them. "It is important that opportunities for using dialogue are not squandered – always make sure that no word is wasted, and that it has a purpose in the story ..."

Writing fiction is like an artist standing in front of a blank canvas. He sees in his mind's eye the focus of the intended painting but often the viewer's eye is often drawn to the tiny

details that make up the background for the main subject. The narrative is the main subject, but the dialogue provides the minute background details that give the whole its fascination. Try these two exercises:

Exercise 1:

The most famous walk-on part in literature is probably that of the Gatekeeper in *Macbeth* but chit-chat and small talk can be utilised to provide background information without the need for long and involved narrative. This can be details provided by a stranger in a train, a publican, postman or any local tradesman, who can walk into the story, deliver the required information and walk out again without leaving any gaps in the continuity. For example:

As the train shuddered to a halt Angie was able to study the castle from a distance. "It's a sinister place, all right," said the man sitting opposite, following her gaze. "Local legend says the hauntings go back to a wicked lord of medieval times but the family's always been a bad lot and a ghost is a convenient way of explaining why so many of them have come to a sticky end."

"I suppose every castle and old family has its ghostly happenings," said Angie for want of something better to say. "Are you local?"

"Born and bred," replied her fellow traveller. "And I'll tell you this, no local will ever go down among the rocks at the foot of the walls, even at low tide for fear of what might happen to them."

Her curiosity thoroughly piqued, Angie cushioned herself against the jerking movements of the train as it slowly began to edge forward again. "Surely that's taking superstition too far, isn't it?"

Before she could elicit any further information, however, the man got to his feet. "My stop, I'm afraid ..."

A brief exchange like this can provide the essential details for a story without the need for interrupting the flow of the narrative in order to provide background. Our characters can hold a conversation with complete strangers, just as we do in real life, but the dialogue serves a purpose without cluttering up the story with superfluous characters.

Exercise 2:
The quintessential British opening gambit about the weather can also tell the reader all they need to know about time and season without sounding like the weather forecast. For example:

"Surprisingly mild and sunny for April, and the hawthorn blossom is amazing this year ..."

"We'd planned a summer barbeque for the start of the school holidays but rain's stopped play..."

"This is what I call an Indian Summer. Hot, sunny and the trees ablaze with colour ..."

"Did you know the saying – that if the scarlet pimpernel has its flowers fully open there will be no rain that day – has been proved accurate 92% of the time?"

Most weather lore originates from within rural or coastal communities and gives us the opportunity to add a bit of local colour to our dialogue without straying away from the narrative.

Chapter Four

Verbal Body Language

Dialogue is often supported by gestures as Desmond Morris points out in *Peoplewatching*. Did you know that by the age of two a child can already use nearly 300 words; by three it has tripled this figure; by four it can manage nearly 1600; by the age of five it has a vocabulary of more than 2000 words – all learned at an astonishing rate.

"But despite the possession of an unparalleled communication system, the old visual signals persist and continue to play a vital role. The talking child remains a crying, smiling, laughing child, even though it can speak freely about its emotional conditions. The possession of words adds a whole new dimension to human interactions, but it does not replace the old one."

Linda M James made a similar important observation about body language for when writing dialogue:

"Your protagonist may have a favourite saying/swear word/exclamation that is his trademark. He may resort to clichés or use proverbs. However, while he is talking, he will seldom remain still. He will often use body language to indicate his frame of mind. He may make faces, move his body awkwardly or speak in a particular tone of voice."

Get into the habit of people watching. Observe a group of listeners in a crowded room and it quickly becomes apparent whether they are agreeing or disagreeing with the speaker. The meaning behind nodding the head depends on its tempo; slow nodding conveys agreement, while quick nodding signals enthusiastic agreement, or impatience and a desire to move the conversation along. Head-shaking also conveys different messages, depending upon the rapidity of the movement; when the head is shaken rapidly it reveals that the listener disagrees with the speaker. A slow shaking of the head, however, can convey completely different meanings – exasperation incredulity, disbelief, denial. For example: "You really believe that!" said James, shaking his head slowly in disbelief, compared with "How can you believe that?" asked Brian with a rapid shake of his head.

Other movements can be used to convey the thoughts of your characters such as the folding of the arms, pressing the lips together firmly, placing a hand or finger over the mouth, raising an eyebrow, sighing or looking away. The way people stand during a conversation is also indicative of mood or reaction. As Linda M James points out, people talk to impart information, to ask questions, to express emotion or opinion, to influence or persuade, to discover things, give advice, or just to hear the sound of their own voice. And each one of these reasons will be accompanied by its own gesture or 'tell' because no one remains absolutely motionless when they are speaking.

In this extract from *House of Strange Gods* the protagonists are physically sparring with each other, despite the fact that they remain seated throughout the exchange. The journalist's body language conveys to the Professor that his motives might not be what they seem on the surface:

Gilmour removed a small newspaper cutting from his briefcase and handed it to her. "I saw this and it intrigued me, I just followed it up and made further inquiries." 'Ghostbusters smash bogus magic circle' had been the caption for two column-inches in a tabloid that had sparked his curiosity. "The more I read, the more fascinated I became, and fortunately the *Telegraph's* features editor agreed." His fingers smoothed the fabric of his sleeve.

"I thought your normal approach was to debunk historical myths and expose gullibility, rather than a foray into the realms of parapsychology?" Professor de Foresta made no attempt to glance at the cutting, or remove her gaze from his face.

"It is, but I wanted to do something different with it. I love the research and separating the fact from the fiction; the fact often being much more interesting than the fiction. Besides ... isn't that what you do?" Gilmour's hands continued to betray his nervousness.

Aliona de Foresta inclined her head slightly before replying. "And you don't think that our illustrious dead should be allowed to rest in peace?"

"If they *are* illustrious, but all too often it's proved to the contrary."

"I'm always afraid that retrospective history isn't as fair as it might be. After all how can *we* judge the mind-set of a Stone Age hunter, a 14th century sergeant at arms, or know what Nelson really was thinking at Trafalgar? Besides, I think the world is desperately short on heroes as a result of all these exposes, and prefer to judge by the light of the times, not on the current research of a MA Hons who has never fired a shot in anger, so to speak."

The antagonism is almost palpable and the dialogue conveys the mental image of two dogs in defensive mode: ears erect and stiff-legged. The wrong word or gesture and any chance of peaceful settlement will be gone. Most natural dialogue has 'movement' and must develop naturally to slot seamlessly into the story, which means we must avoid having our characters saying things that are completely out of character – unless it is relevant to the story.

There are also semi-conscious gestures that people make which speak volumes. When Richard Todd addressed the squadron in the film *The Dambusters*, he emphasises the importance of the mission by assuming the stance of 'arms akimbo' – hands on the hips and elbows jutting out. Edward Fox does the same in *A Bridge Too Far*. For example: 'Arms akimbo he addressed the squadron: "The successful completion of this mission will have a drastic effect on the outcome of the war!"' It conveys domination, aggression and command without another descriptive word being written.

In *The Book of Tells*, Peter Collett informs us that during the 16th-17th centuries this gesture was a recognisable posture of the upper-class male, giving Holbein's famous portrait of Henry VIII as a good example. "At the time the arms akimbo posture was intimately connected with the profession of arms – so much so that those who wanted to pass themselves off as having a military background would do so by adopting the posture." The film directors – probably unconsciously – brought the gesture into the 20th-century

The arms crossed posture with the hands tucked away or resting on the inner elbow, signifies defence and defiance and erects a physical barrier between people. Nearly everyone uses this gesture at some stage when they want to cut themselves off from a conversation without physically leaving the group. We often see it used in television crime series when someone is being interviewed by the police in connection with their investigations. 'Arms crossed, Damien sat back in his chair: "What makes you think I had anything to do with it?"' It could be pure bravado but the posture is a defensive movement.

The crossed arms of a self-hugging posture on the other hand suggests insecurity or submissiveness. One example given by Collett is where the hands cross over the chest to grip the bicep of the opposite arm, or gripping the opposite shoulders. This is a self-comforting gesture and we often see it used in drama when the character is a victim; someone who has suffered some form of emotional, mental or physical trauma. 'Greta's crossed hands gripped her upper arms, hugging herself to shut out the pain: "He's dead, isn't he?"'

In *Gestures*, Desmond Morris points out that all of us use hundreds of expressive movements every day, and that each of these actions has a particular history – sometimes personal, sometimes cultural and sometimes more deeply biological.

> "Gestures have quite wrongly been considered a trivial, second-class form of human communication. Because verbal exchanges are man's crowning glory, all other forms of contact are viewed as somehow inferior and primitive. Yet social intercourse depends heavily on the actions, postures, movements and expressions of the talking bodies. Where communication of changing moods and emotional states is concerned, we would go so far as to claim that gestural infor- mation is even more important than verbal. Words are good for facts and for ideas, but without gestures, human social life would become a cold and mechanical process."

So we have it from the expert on human behaviour that gestural communication can, under certain circumstances, be more important than a verbal exchange. By integrating the element of verbal body language into our dialogue we are going quite a lot further along the road of 'showing' not 'telling'.

Accompanying gestures are either symbolic, emblematic, or mimicry. If a person becomes excited during a conversation, they will begin to wave their hands or arms about, gesticulating wildly, often beating time to their words and emphasising the point being made. These gestures are "not performed consciously or deliberately, are largely unidentified and unnamed, and are difficult to recall" because although the person would be conscious that they were using gestures to illus- trate a point they will unable to describe the movements or say why they were making them. If however, a person taps their temple with their forefinger, it implies that the person they are talking about is 'not all the ticket' or 'eccentric but highly intelligent' – two opposing meanings but understood by the other party to the conversation.

> "An emblematic example differs markedly: a woman crosses the road watched by two young men. One man turns to the other and winks at him; the latter replies by shaking his fingers as if they have been burned by something hot. No word is spoken between them. Here the gestures have replaced speech and, if the young men were asked later what precise gestures they had used, they would be able to recall them and, in the case of the wink, actually name one of them." *Gestures*, Desmond Morris.

Mimicry has also entered the language in that we mime the raising of a glass to indicate we are thirsty, or to offer someone a drink across a crowded bar; the thumb and little figure splayed out and held to the ear means 'phone me', or 'I'll phone you' – and will be understood almost anywhere in the world.

With the popularity of 'foreign' movies and television series, we have become familiar with these expressive gestures from all over the world; and many of the movements have extended their use across linguistic and international boundaries. There were 20 key gestures included in Morris's book of that name and the majority can be utilised by novelists to embellish dialogue. For example:

The Fingertip Kiss: How often do we see this gesture where the tips of the fingers of the right hand are pressed together and touched to the lips; the hand is then tossed lightly into the air. This happens frequently on *Strictly Come Dancing* when judge Brun Tonioli gets over-excited about a dancer's performance. It's a gesture of appreciation or 'an exuberant moment of praise for something tasty or beautiful' although its history goes back to the courtly goings-on of the Elizabethan age.

The Fingers Crossed: The crossing of the fingers is a gesture of protection, especially when telling a lie when the crossed fingers are hidden behind the back. If we write:' "I've never seen the woman before!" said Stewart crossing his fingers behind his back', the readers is being shown that he is lying without the need for any further detail.

The Nose Thumb: A childish gesture of mockery although some adults will use it having been reprimanded by a superior. It is an act of defiance in order to keep face in front of colleagues. It may be a trivial gesture today but it has a very long history.

The Hand Purse: With the thumb and four fingers tips brought together as though holding a small object in the palm of the hand. Often seen as very much an Italian gesture, it represents a query or request for the speaker to be precise and implies a certain degree of impatience, especially if the hand is moved in time with each word.

The Cheek Screw: This is an Italian gesture of praise where the straightened finger is pressed against the cheek and the hand rotated. In a small part of southern Spain, however, it means someone is considered effeminate and could cause confusion if made by an Italian to a Spaniard, or vice versa!

The Eyelid Pull: A gesture meaning 'be alert' or 'watch out!' made by the finger pulling down the lower eye lid. Often seen on television being used by characters in pubs when they want to convey "I keep my eyes open, I know things but I ain't telling."

The Forearm Jerk: The clenched fist is jerked forcibly upwards, with the other hand holding down the upper arm. It is obviously meant as a sexual insult along the lines of "Up yours!" and is primarily anal, rather than genital; dominant 'ladettes' will use the gesture to both subordinate males and females.

The Flat-hand Flick: A predominantly southern Mediterranean gesture that means 'Go away!' when the right hand is held with the thumb uppermost and the fingers stretched out and the left hand making a chopping motion to the right wrist. It can also be used to mean 'I'm off!' The vehemence of the gesture is contained within the tone of the conversation.

The 'OK' Gesture: A universal gesture with the thumb and forefinger touching to make a circle to indicate that something is good or okay; from precision and approval to agreement and praise.

The Vertical Horn Sign: The hand held with the forefinger and little finger extended upwards. Morris describes this as "as gross insult of a special kind with a long and ancient history", and although it is the sign of the cuckold with a dominant message of impotence and stupidity, it is probably best suited to period dialogue of the historical novelist rather than contemporary writing. Although not obsolete it would certainly be considered old-fashioned unless used as a joke.

The Horizontal Horn Sign: The hand pointed forward with the forefinger and little finger extended horizontally. An ancient gesture some 2500-years old and usually made as a gesture casting or protection from the Evil Eye. "By making the sign of the horns, the gesturer was supposed to be able to defend himself against evil spirits ..." The opposite meaning is

"I am putting the evil eye on you", or wishing ill-luck to befall the victim.

The Fig: The hand is closed so that the tip of the thumb protrudes from between the first and second fingers to represent female genitalia. The gesture appears to have several meanings but general used as a sexual insult: "She is an easy lay" or casting aspersions on the masculinity of someone. Amulets depicting this gesture are sold as charms to avert the evil eye.

The Head Toss: This gesture involves the head being tossed smartly upwards and backwards in a short jerk to signify a beckoning movement with an element of command: "Outside!"

The Chin Flick: The backs of the fingers of one hand are flicked forwards in an arc, brushing against the underside of the chin is a gesture of disinterest or dismissive. This is rather a rude or ill-mannered gesture and seeming used to convey the verbal messages of: "I have had enough of you," "What a nuisance!" or "You are boring me to death!"

The Cheek Stroke: The thumb and forefinger placed one on each cheek-bone and gently stroked downwards usually means that someone is looking thin and ill. The gesture would be made behind a person's back and used to ask the silent question: "What on earth is wrong with John? He looks awful."

The Thumb Up: The thumb held vertically erect over a clenched hand is another universally recognisable gesture for OK. "The thumbs-up sign as George came out of court, told me that everything had gone according to plan."

The Teeth Flick: The thumb-nail placed behind the lower edge of the upper front teeth and jerked forward making a clicking sound is an arrogant and dismissive gesture, and one that is used by some tempestuous Latin beauty to show her scorn or anger. As Morris points out, the mood is unpleasant, and the gesture a deliberately unfriendly one.

The Ear Touch: The ear being deliberately touched can be a warning that someone is listening to a conversation; or that someone should listen to what is being said around them.
It can mean "Keep your mouth shut!" or "Listen to what that man next to you is saying!"

The Nose Tap: The forefinger placed vertically along the nose and then gently tapping it is generally a gesture of complicity meaning "It's a secret" or "Keep quiet about it".

The Insult V-Sign: The ubiquitous V-sign made from the forefinger and middle finger raised with the palm towards the gesturer's face means: "Fuck you!" as opposed to the Churchillian Victory sign with the palm facing outwards. The insult-V is a derisive gesture and appears to have been around from the 16th-century but it was brought kicking and screaming into the 20th-century when show jumper Harvey Smith used the gesture to convey the message "Up you!" to the owner of the Hickstead course in 1971.

A similar insulting gesture that has grown in popularity in the 20th-century is **The Raised Middle Finger** which conveys similar sentiments but didn't appear to be around in 1981 when Desmond Morris first published *Gestures*. Nevertheless, it is a widely used gesture in the 2000s and reminds us that even gestures conform to fashion when it comes to using verbal body language in our writing.

Only twenty years ago it was considered affected for someone to 'talk with their hands' and for those of us who naturally used our hands to illustrate a point, we were often told to stop waving our hands about. The French and the Italians did it but it was frowned upon as 'another one of those filthy foreign habits'. It is now acceptable for presenters on television to wave their arms around when delivering the news – good or bad. In fact, it seems that nowadays everyone gesticulates when they are talking, regardless of whether the gesture has any real meaning or not. Try these two exercises:

Exercise 1:
There are all sorts of ways of describing someone's behaviour or reaction via the use of dialogue that offers the opportunity for creating some wonderful visual pictures with the clever use of similes. In *Bone Idle*, Suzette M Hill has the dog commenting on the cat's offended sensibilities: *"But of course the cat doesn't see the funny side of it at all – which is why he is now crouched under the apple tree looking like the Wrath of God."* A perfect thumb-nail sketch of incandescent rage if ever there was one!

The Masters of the casual use of similes are still undoubtedly Raymond Chandler and P G Wodehouse but the less literary have managed to come up with some beauties in their time.

Such as the football commentator who observed that: *"Patrick Thistle took the field today like Boadicea out to take on the Romans"* [*The Book of Similes*, Robert Baldwin and Ruth Paris] or Prince Charles commenting on presenting press awards: *"I feel rather like a pheasant giving out prizes to the best shots."*

On the proper creation of similes, Raymond Chandler, said that the writer should concentrate on whatever is being described rather than diverting attention to the vehicle of comparison.

Exercise 2:

Select one of the key-gestures above and write a short piece of dialogue including the appropriate body language. For example: **The 'OK' Gesture:** A universal gesture with the thumb and forefinger touching to make a circle to indicate that something is good or okay; from precision and approval to agreement and praise.

> Stephen raised his hand with its thumb and forefinger touching to signal that everything was okay. His gesture was discreet compared to Ryan punching the air and shouting 'Yes!' at the top of his voice. "I told you everything would be fine," he whispered to Laura. "Let Ryan draw attention to himself, he'll regret it later when the press latches on to him."

The more obtuse the key-gesture the more an explanation is needed for the reader's benefit.

Chapter Five

Interview and Interrogation

Interviewing and interrogating are all about asking questions – often the sort of question the reader will be asking in their own mind if we don't satisfy this need in our narrative. Author of historical romances and adult fiction, Kelly Lawrence, had this to say on the subject:

"If you put the words 'erotic' and 'dialogue' together in the same sentence chances are some phrases will pop to mind that wouldn't sound out of place in the repertoire of an adult phone line worker. Erotic scenes can often trip up the most experienced writers when it comes to authentic dialogue and so many writers avoid it altogether. For this reason in many erotic scenes main characters, even the most loquacious, suddenly become very quiet. Erotic interludes can go on for hours without any of the participants murmuring so much as a 'left a bit darling.'

This is a shame, because well-crafted dialogue, used at the right moments, can add depth and authenticity to your characters erotic encounters as well as ensuring they remain pivotal to the story rather than seeming separate from them. As I argue in my guide to writing erotic scenes '*Passionate Plots*' any sex scenes, regardless of genre and explicitness, should serve to move the story forward in some way and should be an integral part of the plot. Tacky or non-existent dialogue can pull the reader out of the story as well as making erotic moments seem superfluous."

Sexy scenes don't just occur in erotica and romance novels, they crop up all over the place in thrillers, westerns, science fiction, historical adventure – after all, where would Bernard Cornwell's *Sharpe* series be without a few sexy scenes to enliven the narrative. Kelly Lawrence continues:

"So what should your characters be saying? The first thing to ask yourself is, what *would* they say? By the time you get round to being comfortable enough with your characters to get them naked together, you should know them well enough to have a good idea of the way they would express themselves in this situation. And it's not just about talking dirty; as I also state in *Passionate Plots*, if your lead female character is generally incredibly well spoken and quite reserved, it's highly unlikely that in the bedroom she will suddenly morph into auditioning from *Debbie Does Dallas*. So let your characters lead you.

Also, think about why they are having sex right now, at this particular point in the story. Erotic scenes are an excellent way to deepen your characterisation and reveal more of your protagonists to the reader. As dialogue remains one of the pivotal ways to 'show, rather than tell' a well-timed sentence or short exchange can reveal a great deal about how your characters are feeling. Rather than telling your reader that John felt over awed by Jane's naked beauty, for example, he can say 'My God, you're beautiful,' or even a simple 'wow' as Jane unrobes, or whatever words would best suit your character. Sex scenes aren't always Hollywood style romance either; a giggled comment or in-joke between the characters at the right time can perfectly illustrate moments of awkwardness, shyness or even intimacy. Tenderness can also be evoked in just a few words. In the following short extract from my New Adult romance '*Unconditional*' (Lodestone Books, Feb 2014) the characters have just made love for the first time;

We touch each other for a while longer, exploring each other, and I soon forget my shyness, losing myself in each new sensation. I feel kind of awkward and fumbly, it's no Hollywood movie or even a scene from one of my romances, but somehow everything is just right. After a while we stop and he pulls himself up on his hands, leaning over me.

'Do you want to?' he asks, and I nod, biting my lip.

'You're sure? Because I don't want to rush you.'

'Sssh,' I say, 'I'm sure.'"

In *Write A Western in 30 Days*, Nik Morton also touched on the subject of introducing sex into the equation by giving just sufficient visual information in *The $300 Man* to aid the reader without being too graphic:

"Tomorrow honey, it will all be over," Corbin said, cupping her melon-shaped breasts and kissing them. A light scent of lemon verbena clung to her skin.

"It's a dangerous game you play," she whispered, running a finger over the welts in his shoulder.

"With you – or the Walkers?"

"Oh, the Walkers. This is no game we play, darling Corbin. This is serious." She kissed him and for the second time this night they made love...

By contrast, this sequence in *House of Strange Gods*, is suggestive, a foregone conclusion, and injects an element of humour into what might have been just yet another turgid seduction.

It follows a revelation that Aliona's son had dived into the moat at the family home and swum round to his wife's bedroom because she'd jokingly said that he wasn't romantic anymore.

"I'm glad to know that Luc's inherited some of his father's impetuosity," mused Aliona as they watched Katy hurry down the tree-lined path towards the harbour.

"With your family history I would have thought he was

well advised to keep away from water," retorted Richard. "How would it impress you if I scaled the terraces in the middle of the night to reach your bedroom?"

"It would be a completely futile exercise when all you have to do is walk up the stairs," replied Aliona with a throaty chuckle as she returned to her study.

"With that bloody dog of yours around?" Richard called after her good naturedly but a crafty look came over his face; he'd see whether his sister-in-law by marriage really liked impetuosity.

Later that night Aliona was sprawled out across the bed when she became aware that there was someone moving stealthily in the darkness. "Anubis?" she whispered.

"He can sleep on my bed tonight," answered Richard's voice. "Now shut up and move over!" An answering muffled bark of complaint came from the floor below.

All through the construction of the novel we need to constantly ask ourselves questions about our characters' behaviour. Are they running true to form? Would they *really* have said that in any given situation? Are we putting words into their mouths to fill space, or is the conversation really pertinent to the development of the plot? In turn our characters need to question each other. Why are they there? How much should each of them reveal by that point in the story? Who should keep a secret, and who should reveal it? Are the characters themselves pertinent to the story?

The use of dialogue in scenes of gratuitous violence and high drama must also be 'convincing' for the reader, if not necessarily 100% accurate. Even the most disciplined, blue-bloodied, former Sandhurst cadet isn't going to say: "Pass me the grenade, old chap, if it's not too much trouble?" Like the rest of his men, he's more likely to shout: "Hand me that fucking grenade, Corporal!" when they're under attack and the situation is desperate. Although the saying 'to swear like a barrack army sergeant' has passed into the language it can be extremely boring for the reader if the dialogue consists of repetitive expletives – even if that is what happens in real life warfare.

Clive Cussler manages to blend non-stop drama with testosterone-laden jargon: as the blurb for *Skeleton Coast* tells us this 'is an assault of pulse-pounding action and heart-stopping thrills'. And yet the dialogue – even between male and female combatants – lacks nothing in terms of excitement. We don't stop to think: "Would those mercenaries *really* talk like that?" because the non-stop action sweeps us along using dialogue to inform the reader what's about to happen next, rather than relying on narrative description.

All these questions relate to credibility and often give clues to the sub-text or sub-plot that runs in tandem with the main plot to provide the opportunity for additional conflict, red herrings and mystery. For example: in a recent SF thriller one of the characters was heard to mutter her thoughts aloud by another during their first meeting: "So that's why we've both been included on this mission..." It conveys to the reader that character Number One has sussed something out ahead of the others, and that there's an element of mystery involved which isn't to do with the main plot.

In *How To Write and Sell Great Short Stories* Linda M James tells us: "Writers with a 'good ear' for dialogue will be able to write conversations in such a way that the reader will understand the sub-text, i.e. the thing that the speaker is really speaking about or hinting at. Also, it will not be necessary, in a good piece of dialogue, to describe how the writer is delivering the speech. For instance, "I'm leaving!" she said impatiently, could be written "I've had it! I'm off!" We don't need the adverb 'impatiently'." Try these two exercises:

Exercise 1

Asking questions is a tried and tested method of moving a story along or condensing the narrative, because you're having your character(s) asking the questions about something that might be puzzling or confusing to your reader – the point being clarification.

"But I still don't understand *how* you knew she wasn't a genuine witch?" said Gemma.

"Because no real witch is going to keep banging on about black and white witches," replied Stella. "Or name-dropping the way she did. The one thing that any genuine witch knows about and that's 'keeping silence'. It just not done to talk about other witches by name to outsiders."

"She could just have been showing off," said Benjie mulishly, still smarting from the fact that *he'd* been taken in from the beginning. "She was very good at reading the tarot. Lots of things she told me were correct."

"She had merely memorised the standard interpretations of the Marseilles deck and could trot out the reading quite glibly," said Stella. "She had the fortune-teller's instinct reading body language, and knew quite a lot about your family background before you asked for a reading. The rest was easy."

"When did you start to suspect things weren't quite right?" asked Gemma.

"When she told Benjie that he couldn't escape his fate," said Stella. "The future *isn't* fixed. The tarot reveals the future as relating to the past and the present, and what will happen if the warnings aren't heeded in order to change things *before* they go wrong. The direction of the trouble or change is influenced by the cards on either side, which give you 'intelligence' of the evasive or preparatory action needed to be taken. Benjie's reading was given as a *fait accompli* – it could not be undone. Which was utter rubbish!"

Here we have imparted information that would have required a lot more detail if it had been included as part of the narrative text. By using dialogue we cut to the chase and give a sharp, concise explanation without burdening the reader with too much information.

Exercise 2

One of the most frequent questions asked in novel writing workshops is how far should the novelist be expected to go in order to give a typescript the right amount of sex-appeal. The answer is, of course, how good are you at writing about it? Recently, in an idle moment, I picked up a second-hand paperback from a charity shop that promised to expose the sexy secrets of Hollywood society and in a double page spread, nine people were committing some sexual indiscretion in six different locations. (I'll leave you to work out the permutations but I assure you the author convinced me that it was possible.) A mainstream publisher had accepted it, but do authors really enjoy writing that sort of stuff if their chosen genre isn't erotica? I suspect not. Explicit sex is often unnecessary and boring, and reeks of "the faint aroma of performing seals" rather than Chanel No.5 and if the dialogue isn't spontaneous, then the whole thing becomes an embarrassment.

Frederick Forsyth did it extremely well when writing *The Day of The Jackal* and obviously felt compelled to add seduction to the talents of the character who was so obviously '100% male', that to not to have mentioned it would have been sacrilege. The result was a beautifully erotic 300-word bedroom scene that should have left any red-blooded female demanding an email address – if an overzealous police commissaire hadn't been so meticulously efficient with half a magazine of 9mm bullets from a MAT49 carbine. Forsyth's novel carried a first-class story and needed no extra 'spice' to liven it up.

Mills & Boon characters are now doing it with impunity after all the years of straight-laced narrative, and many of the other mainstream publishers have erotica as one of their imprints. So even if the best selling lists are no longer dominated by sexy (often a euphemism for 'tasteless') books, then obviously novelists can dispense with the impulse to add a bit of spice purely for titillations sake. Study the 'sexy bits' in the latest novels and see how the author tackles the question of sexy dialogue. In *Passionate Plots* Kelly Lawrence offers good advice on how to integrate sexy scenes into non-erotic writing.

Chapter Six

Audience

When we tell a story the reader becomes our audience and as any speaker or stand-up comedian will tell you, it is necessary to engage with an audience for the performance to go well. The writer could be well advised to take this advice on board. Very often we need to use dialogue to tell a story within a story so that the reader has instant access to the background details that otherwise would require the novel's narrative to cover a much longer time-span, and often dispenses with the need for lengthy 'flash-backs' or reverie. This is where we become a story-teller within our own story.

By using characters in the present-day story as an audience, the narrator involves them in the events from the past by having them ask the questions that may not be immediately clear to the reader. In other words, the listener requests clarification of certain points for the purpose of continuity within the story line. By asking 'What do you mean?' or 'I don't understand' the speaker is forced to make explanations for his audience's benefit. If our character *deliberately* hedges then there is the suggestion of an untruth that must be uncovered later in the story. It's all part of the weaving of the plot.

Thriller writer John Connolly uses this technique in *The Burning Soul* when private investigator, Charlie Parker, and a lawyer, listening to the account of a convicted child-killer, retell the story of how he and another 14-year old boy murdered a young girl many years before. Parker and the lawyer are *his* audience; his narrative vacillating between minimising his own role on the events and a web of finely strewn lies. The listeners rarely interrupt but *their* body language plays a contributing factor in the dialogue; the speaker is constantly forced to explain himself in more detail in order to obtain sympathy and support from them.

In *Riptide,* Lincoln Preston uses a three-way dialogue to tell the story of the pirate's treasure via an encrypted 17th-century journal, which involves an antiquarian, a computer whizz-kid, and the owner of the island on which the buried treasure is supposedly located. The dialogue quickly reveals the rivalry between traditional research methods and computer-analysis with its techno-jargon used to rile the historian who doesn't understand it. For the benefit of the reader/audience the owner of the island doesn't understand either of them, and it is he who constantly asks 'Can you explain that in layman's terms?' The technique continues throughout the novel because the code is being broken as the narrative progresses – even switching to a second Elizabethan code that is even more complex – which requires more lengthy explanation/discussion between the three characters.

I used the same technique in *House of Strange Gods* to introduce the reader to a character's history, while he was cementing a bond with two other members of the Charter House team. It gave as much background as the reader needs to know at that point in the story without having to go back in time to trawl for irrelevant details – and delay the action with lengthy character descriptions.

The former soldier was distinctly unhappy in his latest assignment among people he thought were downright weird. He'd been considered a tough but fair officer by his men, and had seen quite a lot of action prior to being moved into military intelligence; even then, he had still been exposed to a certain amount of danger until that damned bullet had put paid to his career. Now he was stuck here with these intellectual kooks and psychics because the powers that be thought his 'new skills' were too useful to allow him to be discharged.

"C'mon man, chill a bit. This isn't MI6 here, no spooks, or

wire taps. Just hot sunshine, cold beer and a compliant woman catering for your every need."

"Another crack like that and you'll be in the harbour, Daws," retorted Chris putting down a tray of enormous man-sized sandwiches and handing Andy a beer. "So how are you settling in?" she asked, "I expect it's different to the Army and ... whatever you were in."

"Yeah. I don't even know what I'm doing here. I mean, no disrespect but you lot are all ... well, *what* exactly are you?"

"Just spooks of a different kind," said Jack with a grin. "So how did you land up here? I mean, you're still regular Army from what Aliona told us, former Hereford mob and ex-Intelligence. Not exactly what we're used to either." There was a challenge in the dark eyes but no hint of malice.

"Jack!!"

"No, it's okay Chris," answered Andy. "When you work as a team you have to know who everyone is, and whether you can depend on them if you get in a tight spot. I guess I don't feel part of the team because there's nothing here I can relate to. I mean that back there ..." he nodded his head in the direction of the Charter House. "... That's just police work if you remove the esoteric stuff."

"It's 'stuff' that can't be allowed to get into the public domain for a variety of reasons," responded Chris. "Similar, I'm sure, to what you've been used to dealing with. This can be classed as terrorism of a different kind, but it still has to be dealt with."

"But why are *you* here?" Jack persisted. At last they were having a productive conversation with this taciturn former army Captain, and he was beginning to feel good about the outcome.

"I took a bullet in the head on my last assignment, and was in a coma for two months. When I came out of it, I'd developed the ability to read minds. Which is a perfect asset for an Intelligence Officer, but not for one with the bullet still lodged in his brain; I was deemed unfit for *active* duty, and too valuable to retire. I was given a political assignment to look after some big wig on safari but I blotted my copy book ... and here I am."

"Oooh, I do love gossip. Do tell," said Chris.

"Not really gossip. It was a camera safari with a production team specialising in filming wild life. They'd set up where the wildebeest cross a crocodile infested river and waited for the action. One poor animal was attacked by this big bastard of a croc and the director ordered the camera to keep filming. Then he commented that the fight could last for anything up to half an hour before it was all over. The guy I was supposed to be minding started a book on how long the wildebeest would take to die – and we're talking thousands!"

"Go on."

"Not only can I read minds, I've found that I also lock into emotion and all I could feel was that animal's raw, primordial fear washing over me in great waves. It was *me* down there fighting for my life with every ounce of strength I had – and I knew I was going to lose. Those two bastards were laughing about the inevitability of it and actually enjoying the struggle. I just snatched the rifle from the attendant 'Great White Hunter' and made the shot. I was nearly lynched for spoiling their fun and ruining the filming – about 10 seconds of television time!"

Jack studied the flecks of sunlight reflected in the water for a moment before saying anything. "Tell you what Andy. If we ever find ourselves in a situation where my death is inevitable, promise me you'll not hesitate to make that shot." He put out his hand and the soldier took it in his firm grip.

"Funny," he said finally. "Aliona said exactly the same thing." He suddenly realised that although Jack Daws might act the fool, he was someone you could rely on to stand at your back in a tight corner. Perhaps life among these nutters might not be so bad after all.

Telling a story in this manner reveals the personal nature of the three psychic investigators and that there's a bond already beginning to form. Andy's plight tells us that although he's floundering like a fish out of water among strangers, he is a very tough and capable soldier. When Jack and Chrissie later suggest he accompany them on a climbing weekend, we know that the bond will be sealed because they've agreed to meet on common ground. We also realise without a word being said that Chrissie is as tough as her two male companions.

We can also embellish our story-telling by utilising folklore and superstitions to add an element of mystery even in a non-mystery novel. *The Penguin Guide to the Superstitions of Great Britain and Ireland* can provide endless material for adding local colour to a story. Every location in the world will have its own 'native' folk-tales and these can be told by casual 'walk-on' characters who have no other part to play in the narrative – a stranger met in a bar or on a train who imparts a small piece of local history or superstition – and then takes his (or her) leave quite naturally.

Clive Cussler brings all these elements into play in *Inca Gold* when a group of archaeologists and a team of explorers sit around a camp fire during a mission to track down stolen artefacts. The conversation is lengthy but it involves different specialists adding their 'four-penny worth' to provide a solid background to the adventure. Here the characters are *telling* the story of the treasure they're looking for in the process of *showing* how dangerous and arduous their investigation is going to be.

In *The Perk*, novelist Mark Gimenez doesn't waste time describing the assets of the 800 acre ranch, he has the owner give his long-lost son and grandson a conducted tour, and the dialogue between the three generations provides the reader with all the information they need to know in order to be able to visualise the setting. The visitors' private thoughts add an extra dimension to the three-way conversation in revealing the tension that exists between them.

Some writing tutorials will discourage the use of clichés but they *are* a popular and familiar part of everyday speech, and convey *exactly* what a character has in mind; just as in real-life dialogue, a speaker will often mix metaphors. Where we can have a little bit of fun is having our characters create their own similes, such as Raymond Chandler's famous complimentary: '*She was a blonde to make a bishop kick a hole in a stained glass window*' or Martin Amis's less complimentary '*N ... dirty little fingers rifle through his subject's private life like a hick detective investigating a pimp's account book*' quoted in *The Book of Similes* by Robert Baldwin and Ruth Paris.

There are numerous ways of livening up dialogue and although it should always serve a purpose that doesn't mean to say it can't be amusing, entertaining or instructive at the same time. Think of yourself in the reader's position and read the dialogue aloud to see if it gels with the characters who are delivering it. It's a piece of advice that many writing tutors and authors will offer but it's something that amateur novelists ignore. When checking your passages of dialogue try to think like a scriptwriter and visualise the conversation taking place on a television screen and ask yourself critically: 'Does it work?' Try these two exercises:

Exercise 1:
Select a piece of local superstition or folklore and tell the story by using dialogue between two or three people. Take for example the entry inspired by Glamis Castle in *A Companion to the Folklore, Myths & Customs of Britain* by Marc Alexander. It doesn't have to be a real castle in your narrative...

"Glamis Castle not only has the reputation of being the world's most haunted castle but it also has the widest range of legends associated with it. Our brief is to investigate the alleged psychic disturbances that apparently occur quite regularly," said James Kilroy, "and hopefully contribute to the production of a half-way decent television programme."

"Are we delving into the historical happenings before or after we set up the monitors?" asked Sally.

"Bags I get Lady Janet and the accusations of witchcraft," interrupted Deborah.

"Okay by me. I much prefer the gruesome murder of the Ogilvies," said Keith. "Sir James can take the legend of the secret chamber and its mysterious occupant."

Here we have a group of characters introducing the subject of why they are visiting a haunted castle, and the purpose behind the visit. This is a standard plot for any good horror or mystery novel, which introduces the subject in brief at the start with more in-depth history and discoveries being revealed as the story develops.

Exercise 2:
Have your character read something from a book or document such as the extract from *Glimpses of the Supernatural* (1875) by Revd F G Lee, also concerning Glamis Castle and which could be incorporated into the conversation by one of the characters. The extract is short enough to be used in the dialogue but it contains all the atmosphere needed to set the tone for a creepy story. For example:

"Let me read you something from one of my grandfather's books," said Laura picking up a slim, leather bound volume and turning to a page marked with a slip of paper. "There is no doubt about the reality of the noises at Glamis Castle. On one occasion, some years ago, the head of the family, with several companions, was determined to investigate the cause. One night, when the disturbance was greater and more violent than usual, and it should be premised strange, weird and unearthly sounds had often been heard, and by many persons, some quite unacquainted with the ill repute of the Castle, his lordship went to the Haunted Room, opened the door with a key, and dropped back in a dead swoon into the arms of his companions; nor could he ever be induced to open his lips on the subject afterwards." She closed the book and looked at Charles with a determined lift of her chin.

Here we are using authentic 19th century words to set the scene for our action and literally putting those words into our character's mouth as part of the dialogue.

Chapter Seven

Confrontation

Confrontation (usually referred to as 'conflict') is an important element in all novels and defined by the dictionary as 'the bringing of people face to face; hostile attitude; opposition'. Every plot needs an element of confrontation to develop the story, hold the reader's attention and add a touch of drama – and without it the novel will not work. Confrontational dialogue is usually a verbal battle of wills – a good example being Margit confronting the man who made her watch her father's execution when she was just seven years old in *The Woman in the Fifth*. Douglas Kennedy has his characters fencing with accusation and denial, evidence and justification, until finally the woman's will breaks that of the ageing intelligence officer.

Confrontation doesn't necessarily have to be part of a dramatic scenario but it can be used to set a scene or give a glimpse of personality, such as the exchanges at the beginning of *The Woman in the Fifth*, between the principal character and a difficult Parisian hotel clerk. It gives the reader a key to the character's circumstances and his general behaviour as he allows the clerk to intimidate and extort money because he is a stranger in a strange land. In fact, throughout the novel, Harry Ricks fairs badly in every confrontation, especially the dreaded police inter-rogation, which is a feature in the majority of crime-thrillers as novelist Maureen Carter explains.

A former BBC 'Newsnight' presenter and, having worked extensively in newspapers, radio and television she still freelances in the business, when she's not busy writing her Bev Morris and Sarah Quinn novels. As a journalist Maureen Carter has worked closely with the police, covering countless crime stories, including several murders. She's also interviewed victims and seen villains sent down, which means she's been on the receiving end of gritty dialogue.

"In my book, good dialogue doesn't mince its words; it should speak for itself and say so much more than what's written on the page. Effortlessly and seamlessly it should reveal character, add information, propel the plot, engage, inform and entertain – all without the reader spotting the joins. If it's clunky or every character sounds the same – go back to the drawing-dialogue board.

"I believe that just as every author ought to have his or her own voice, good dialogue comes down to finding the right voice for every character and that means spot-on word choice, speech pattern and rhythm. The vocabulary an author assigns to a character should speak volumes. A tattooed teenager's not likely to say, 'Spiffing weather, old bean' And a bishop probably wouldn't utter the word 'wicked' to confer a blessing. I read my dialogue aloud, over and over again, and I guarantee the fewer words used, the more meaning they'll convey. In similar brevity vein, my dialogue is almost entirely a speech tag and adverb-free zone. If it (and me) is doing its job properly, readers should know who's talking, how they sound, what sort of mood they're in, who they're speaking to and what they had for breakfast. Okay, the last part's negotiable. But you get the picture?

"Nothing slows down pace more quickly than verbal clutter like: Freddie shouted loudly or Suzy whispered breathily. If the dialogue's tailor-made for each character, readers should know by now that it's Freddie who's not a happy bunny and that Suzie really ought to speak up a little. Besides, '*shouting loudly*' isn't just superfluous, it's tautology to boot."

Carter continues: "If I'm writing a police interview scene (make that any scene), the last words I'd use are: Harry Badman snarled menacingly as he jumped to his feet and knocked the chair over. For one thing, Harry doesn't do cutesy snarls and for another the narrative leading up to the tipping point should mean the reader is in no doubt that Harry isn't one of life's givers.

"And all those words get in the way of the action. How much more effective is it, say, to let the reader spot Harry's jaw flex or imagine the noise as the chair scrapes the tiles?

In crime fiction, dialogue is often confrontational. As I write those sorts of scene, my sentences generally become shorter, the dialogue snappier; I use one-liners, even one-word replies, the odd loud pause; characters might talk over each other or just keep shtum. Apart from adding drama and hiking the tension, in theory the exchanges are becoming more telling. My aim is to slip in important information, vital clues, hoping they're subtle enough to pass under the reader's radar.

"Confounding reader expectation is important too, which is why I make sure my villains aren't out of pantomime or sound like Ray Winstone on sixty-a-day. For instance, I have a character in *Working Girls* called Charlie Hawes. He's a pimp who gives psychopaths a bad name. He's strikingly attractive and he could do voice-overs for silk farms. Here he is being questioned over the murder of two girls. His lawyer's called Viner. The detectives are Byford and Bev. We pick it up towards the end of the session...

'Michelle Lucas, Mr Hawes. What can you tell me about her?' Byford was holding a pen, looking expectantly.

Hawes held out empty palms.

'Cassie Swain, Mr Hawes. What can you tell me about her?' They were still empty.

'How many girls are you grooming, Mr Hawes?'

'I don't do hair, Mr Byford.'

'Do a lot of make-up though don't you, Charlie?' Bev couldn't even fake a smile. She lifted his statement. 'How much of this little lot is fantasy?'

'Shut the—'

'My client has nothing further to add.' Viner laid a restraining arm on Charlie's arm.

Then the heat rises.

Bev sauntered past, dropped a casual, 'How's Vicki, Charlie?'

'Fine.'

Gotcha. She spun round. Apart from profanities, it was the only spontaneous remark he'd uttered during the entire charade. Her broad smile was short-lived.

'At least as far as I know.'

She wanted to wipe the yawn off his face. 'And how far's that, Charlie?'

He was casually picking sleep out of the corner of an eye. 'I vaguely recall the name. She came to me for a job once.'

'As what?'

'Part-time scrubber.' He smiled. 'I had an opening for a cleaner.'

'Oh, yeah?'

'I couldn't take her on of course.'

'Why's that?'

'Didn't like the look of her.' He was eyeing Bev again; bopping him would be a joy.

'Too old for you, Charlie? Schoolgirls more your line?'

'My client—'

'Shut it, Max.'

'So when did you last see her?'

'Months ago.'

'I don't believe you.'

'I don't give a shit.'

'You're lying.'

'Prove it, bint.'

Bev smiled. The veneer of civility was cracking.

But of course, Charlie's discomfort doesn't last long.

'Chill, Max. Let them run their little checks. I'm in no hurry.

Make sure you're recording it all for the case, though.'

Bev glanced at the brief. He clearly wasn't up to speed either. 'Case?'

Charlie outlined it slowly. 'Police harassment. Defamation. Perverting the course of justice.'

Bev snorted. That was rich. That was rolling in it.

"And for writers, good dialogue is worth its weight in gold," concludes Maureen Carter.

Surprisingly, confrontational dialogue is usually accompanied by very little body language as the above extract demonstrates and a lot of deceit. Peter Collett cites the narrowing of the eyes in this battle of wills similar to the method used by Clint Eastwood and Lee Van Cleef in *The Good, the Bad and the Ugly*, or the 'closed-mouth smile' that gives the impression that the person on the receiving end is excluded from knowing what's behind the smile.

One of the funniest examples of sustained confrontation is in the *Bones* series of novels by Suzette M Hill during which the principal character – a homicidal vicar – is permanently finding himself in a confrontational situation but with hilarious consequences. Permanently beleaguered by fornicating parishioners, his victim's family, the police, an acerbic sister, and a dubious school chum with 'form' – not to mention a calculating cat and a brain-dead dog – the dialogue throughout the five books is both flowing and amusing.

Confrontation dialogue serves a definite purpose in that it allows the writer to pit two (or more) differing viewpoints against each other to move the story along and to give the reader an opportunity to act as a silent witness to the conversation. One side of the conversation will usually be an accurate account, while the other will be based on lies – and the clever writer knows when to use this device as a red herring! For example Gloria's response reveals that she knows about the missing diamonds but there's a lot more mystery hinted at that Vicky knows nothing about – and probably wouldn't want to know – hence the confrontation between the cousins.

> "It *was* you who stole Aunt Jessie's diamond ring on the day of the funeral, Gloria. I saw you in her bedroom going through her jewellery box but you let Derek take the blame."
>
> Her cousin gave a tight lipped smile, her eyes narrowing. "But I wasn't the only person in the bedroom, Vicky dear. Things aren't always what they seem. You know what you *think* you saw, but that wasn't the whole picture by any means."

We could have used the he said/she said method:

> "You stole Aunt Jessie's ring."
> "No, I didn't."
> "Yes, you did. I saw you ..."

and dragged the dialogue out for pages but the original, using the appropriate body language, is much more punchy and purposeful, in that it introduces a further element of mystery into the proceedings.

According to *The Book of Tells*, a lot of things we tell other people aren't true – they're fibs, fudges, falsehoods, fabrications and barefaced lies. There are lots of ways to convey to a reader that a character is lying and it depends on the importance of the lie in context to the story as to how much is made of it in the text. There are also many reasons why people lie, and not necessarily for personal gain and this fact remains at the heart of the majority of inspirational ideas for novels and story stories. For example:

- White lies to prevent hurt to a person's feelings
- Out of loyalty to another person, family or clan

- To protect someone
- To conceal an important truth
- To throw blame onto someone else
- Fear of deception
- Fear of punishment or retribution
- To gain advancement
- To conceal the past
- To conceal plans for the future

Lies and deceit are an integral part of human relationships – from a kindly response to "Does my bum look big in this?" to the international political leader denying that the troops invading a neighbouring country are under his control. From: "A little inaccuracy sometimes saves tons of explanation (Saki) to: "The greater the lie, the greater the chance that it will be believed," (Adolf Hitler). The way we deal with these scenarios in our fiction can be used as character 'tells' because the way they speak reveals the kind of person they are. The words we put into their mouths reveals just as much as 'tells' can give us an insight into real life people: confrontation is inevitable.

"I subscribe to the Bergan Evans' philosophy that lying is an indispensible part of making life tolerable," said Stephen, with an affected air of world-weariness.

I was more than a little disconcerted to hear this, since this was the man who was marrying my sister in six weeks time, which in turn would give him a foot in the door to the Hamilton family's racing-millions. Did Lizzie know that he firmly endorsed bending the truth when it suited him?

People often ignore the clear signs of being lied to because they don't want to admit someone with whom they share a close relationship is deceitful. Honest people bad at spotting dishonesty because they prefer to believe the best of those around them; while highly suspicious people suspect everyone. Some liars have shifty eyes; others increase the intensity of their gaze – with blinking, fidgeting, agitation, covering mouth or touching the nose giving off signs that a lie is in progress.

The dialogue used during confrontation must be very cleverly orchestrated or it becomes unconvincing. Try these two exercises:

Exercise 1:
Gut feeling (or intuition) plays an important role in lie detection. It provides a 'red herring' with which to weave a tapestry of drama and mystery into even the most romantic of plots; it helps to create the tensions and misunderstandings between characters that every novel needs to keep the reader's interest alive. The following two lines, used in a couple of Harlan Coben novels between two detectives, reveal their mutual suspicion of lies but (as yet) without proof and speaks volumes between the pair.

"He's lying."
"Like a rug."

Create a few lines of dialogue between two of your characters to suggest that a third person is not telling the truth about something. What were the tell-tale signs that made each of them suspicious? Incorporate these into the conversation using this almost telepathic rapport.

Exercise 2:
This short piece contains a lot of information in the four lines of dialogue and something similar would make a riveting opening for a short story or novel. We have confrontation, lies and accusation while telling us quite a lot about Stella without wasting words. We know that she is an Irish Catholic but hasn't

been home for a long time and only family duty has brought her here to confront her past in the figure of Father Murphy. Despite her obvious but unspecified abuse at the hands of this man, she is bloody but unbowed.

"Your Mother, God rest her soul, would have had an easier life if you'd not gone traipsing off to England to follow your own selfish ambition and leaving your brother at home," said Father Murphy.

"And she'd have had a *happier* life if she hadn't been hag-ridden by the Church on account of being a single parent. You never let her get up off her knees!" retorted Stella.

"May God forgive you for your blasphemy on the day of your own Mother's funeral," replied the shocked priest.

The hatred she had for this sanctimonious old man descended like an Irish red mist. "And will God forgive *you* for all the children you've abused over the years, Father? I was one of them, or don't you even remember!" Stella spat vicious, grinding out her cigarette in one of her Mother's best saucers.

There are several intricate themes that can be explored within the narrative of the story but there's enough how, why, what, where and when to hook the reader's curiosity even if we never revisit the scene of the exchange.

Try writing an opening sequence composed purely of dialogue to set the scene for your story. Without giving the game away, we can, for example, see why this character has turned her back on her homeland, family and religion – it is up to the author to reveal whether this has made her a better person, or enabled her to escape her roots.

Chapter Eight

Talking To Yourself

Another useful aspect of dialogue is the use of silent thought to convey inner, highly personal details of the character. This often manifests quite successfully as narrative written in the first person, where 'I' tells the story or uses reflection and reverie to move things along. The reader is our audience but we often get the feeling that the narrator is often oblivious to their existence; that the characters are telling the story for their own benefit or amusement. Like Lord Ruthven in *Charnel House Blues: The Vampyre's Tale*, where the narrator shows total disregard for the reader's sensibilities, which is totally in keeping with what we would see as a vampire's perspective:

> "Needless to say, the contacts I'd made during all the Grand Tours stood me in good stead when I reached England. The introductions gave me access to the wives, sweethearts and sisters of those young men whose company I'd sought in Italy, France and Greece. I was considered to be fascinating and exotic, and since the touch of the vampire allowed for seduction without dishonour, I was able to pleasure those young ladies of noble birth in secret. The vampire's kiss is not always deadly, and the smallest sip can be likened to savouring a glass of fine wine, without the urge to consume the whole bottle."

Douglas Kennedy in *The Pursuit of Happiness* uses a similar first-person technique in that his elderly character records the narrative in the form of a typescript created for the daughter of her deceased lover. It is an extended letter to explain circum-stances that had affected all their lives but there is the overall sense that Sara's true reason for writing her account is to enable *herself* to relive the past and exorcise her own ghosts. Kennedy uses this approach again in *The Woman In The Fifth* as the main character tries to work out in his own mind exactly what is happening to him – we, the readers are incidental to his story. In other words, first-person narrative is a useful technique for conveying the inner thought-processes of our characters.

The more common method of showing 'thought' is with the use of italics, for example: *If I have to listen to any more of her matrimonial drivel I'll scream*, thought Beth, her actual words belying her antipathy towards the tennis pro's irritating wife. "Glenda, how lovely to see you ..."

Irish novelist, Tana French used this lavishly in *Broken Harbour* to reflect the turmoil in the mind of a suburban housewife as she descends into madness and murder. And it also spills over into the over-active imagination of the detective investigating the case, as he tries to come to terms mentally with where his investigation will eventually lead.

In *Dead Run* by P J Tracy, italicised thought reflects the mind-set of the FBI profiler who has a deep-seated fear of using her gun against another human being, as and when – as it inevitably will – become necessary. As the tension and drama in the narrative mount, so does the voice of doubt in Sharon's brain, although the italics are fewer and shorter as the novel reaches its conclusion and the woman faces up to her fears.

Sometimes the technique is used to break up a third-person narrative where a whole sequence from a couple of pages to a whole chapter is presented in italic. This leaves the reader in no doubt that there has been a significant switch in character, time and/or place. It should not, however, be used to pad out the narrative to include superfluous and random thought processes and must remain firmly within the confines of the story. Even idle thoughts must serve a purpose as far as the reader is concerned.

Reflection is a 'thought or utterance resulting from contemplation' and in this extract from *The Wild Horseman*, Richard Todhunter's outburst sums up the impossible situation in which he's found himself:

> "I must be bloody mad," he said aloud, tightening the girth on Saladin's saddle. Not only was he, a crippled ex-jockey, attempting to outrun the advancing German army. He was going to take on the responsibility for a psychotic stallion; a green mare (who was likely to come into season just by being in close proximity to Saladin!); a sixteen-year old stable girl, and now a geriatric greyhound, who was sitting there expectantly, waiting for the off. A simpler solution would be to go behind a barn with the revolver and blow his brains out!

The enormity of the task in hand is encapsulated in the man's train of thought but is not without its subtle black humour. While tacking up his horse, these thoughts reveal that he's summing up all the things that could and probably would go wrong during the long trek to the Normandy coast.

Reverie describes 'a mental abstraction; an undirected train of thoughts or fancies in meditation' and in this extract from the Prologue of *The Wild Horseman*, Jenny Malcolm finds her mind drifting back in time:

> Involuntarily, her fingers went to the place on her upper arm where a scar had healed in the shape of a miniature horseshoe. Jonathan had always insisted that she wear sleeves long enough to conceal the wound, *but he'd never been able to suppress the scars of memory that had been etched into my soul, poor man*, she thought sadly. She had been branded by life but it was a scar she would willingly carry to the grave – and never regret for a moment. Even under the fabric of her smartly tailored dress, she could feel the puckered skin of the bullet wound.

Even when our characters are thinking, either aloud or silently, they are dragging the reader along in their wake and moving the story along. In the first extract we are given a catalogue of disasters waiting to happen, while in the Prologue there is the suggestion of pain and danger that has already been encountered and survived. This is a fast-moving adventure story that 'offers opportunity to experience the thrill of a ride that will last a lifetime'.

Barbara Ford-Hammond, publisher of Bedroom Books also endorses the need for dialogue to have meaning, to add to or move the story along and the benefits of reading passages aloud. "Dialogue for the sake of it is a waste of time and not worth the reader's time or effort. I think too many authors try to write dialogue that is grammatically correct when in reality we do not speak like that. It must flow naturally and the words spoken must be in character. Authors should read their work out loud and if it sounds stilted then it is wrong. The dialogue in this extract from *Catching Stars* tells so much ..."

The little girl looked at Eli with her big blue eyes. "Thank you very much." She looked back at her aunt to make sure all was well. When her aunt nodded, she turned back to Eli and put her hand in her other pocket and pulled out another toad, holding it out to him. "I got us both one."

Eli smiled and took the toad from her. "Thank you."

Maggie looked at the adults. "Can we go play now?"

Magdalene smiled. "Of course you can. Go have fun."

Eli looked at his mother who seemed a little worried about the boy in fresh church clothes, after seeing the little girl with dirty hands and feet. "I didn't know they'd be playing outside."

Magdalene smiled. "That's alright. Addie, can you get some play clothes for Mr. Eli?"

Addie smiled, "Course, Miss Magdalene." She waved to

Eli and walked toward the house. "Come on chil', we find you somethin' to play in."

Eli carried his toad and followed Addie inside.

Within minutes, the children were running down toward the creek, barefoot and laughing.

Magdalene looked over at Lizbeth. "I think this is meant to be."

Lizbeth sipped her drink. "What's that?"

The woman smiled at her guest. "I think those two are going to grow up and fall in love. I've seen it in the stars, — and Macy told me."

"Macy?"

Magdalene nodded. "My dead sister, — she's been talking up a storm since her Maggie met your Eli."

There are a lot of unspoken thoughts and feelings in this extract, and with the minimum amount of narrative, the author lets the characters speak for themselves.

Using the technique of silent thought allows us to reveal more about the characters than would normally happen during a conversation and dispenses with the need for lengthy paragraphs describing a character's behaviour. Introspection, which is the 'observation and analysis of the processes of one's own mind' can be far more revealing in a story than relying on a third-person narrative. Try these two exercises:

Exercise 1:
Possibly one of the most chilling fictional 'thoughts' is contained in Agatha Christie's thriller, *Endless Night*, when the murderer reflects on his crime:

"Funny, after she was dead I never thought of Greta much …After I'd killed her she didn't seem to matter anymore … I tried to bring back the splendid triumphant feeling that I'd had when I strangled her. But even that was gone away."

Here we have an economy of words with the maximum effect. The brutality lies, not in the crime but in the total dismissal of the victim as anyone of any consequence. Try writing a similar intro-spective thought by one of your characters in less than 50 words, wherein a 'secret' is reflected upon using the same crisp, analytical style.

Not every novel contains a murder, of course, but any story will benefit from there being a secret of some sort to add a bit of extra spice and drama.

Exercise 2:
Next try an exercise in combining a two-part conversation with italicised thought. In this example there are lots of different undercurrents:

"Are these flowers fresh?" Miss Bloomingdale's voice boomed across the florist shop, startling the other customers into stampeding out of the door.

"Fresh this morning," replied Sarah through gritted teeth.

"I must have fresh flowers for the church," the former headmistress announced. "Unlike Sheila Francis I don't use cut flowers from the garden. The church deserves better, I think."

Unlike you, Sheila Francis knows what she's doing, you old cat, thought Sarah watching the elderly woman thoughtfully running her fingers over the purple heads of the monkshood. *You don't even remember that I'm that little Sarah Lynn you used to bully unmercifully. The girl you said would never amount to anything, and here you are in* my *shop.*

"These would look wonderful as a focal point on the altar ..."

"I wouldn't ..." Sarah attempted to warn her customer that the monkshood was highly toxic.

"Nonsense. The colour is perfect! I'll take a dozen stems."

"A dozen it is," replied Sarah smugly. *And by the time you've finished handling the leaves without wearing gloves, the poison will have been absorbed through the skin. First you'll feel a tingling sensation that will creep up your arm to the shoulder, followed by an unpleasant numbness – after which your heart will start to be affected. It's not called the 'queen of poisons' for nothing.* "Make sure you fluff the leaves up well when arranging them," she added helpfully with a smile.

This little exchange may end in death but we've seen enough of Miss Bloomingdale to realise that she's a thoroughly unpleasant character. Sarah knows her stuff but her victim would never give anyone credit for anything hence her comments about another woman who provides flowers for the church rota. The florist was obviously deeply scarred by the former teacher's acid comments directed at her when she was a child, and can perhaps be forgiven for wanting to get her own back when the position of power is reversed.

By using factual information about the monkshood, we demonstrate that the character has a lot of knowledge about plants and flowers in addition to merely arranging them. Without going into detail, we also realise that the florist might be about to commit murder – although it may not be her actual intention. Or is it? Try writing a similar sequence using your own characters' silent thoughts.

Chapter Nine

Shooting the Breeze –
Accents, Dialect and Other Worlds

It doesn't matter what type of fiction we're writing – the message is loud and clear and as Krystina Kellingley, of Cosmic Egg, the fantasy, horror and science fiction publisher agrees the importance of dialogue cannot be over emphasized.

"Dialogue, both internal and external *is* your character. It's the medium by which your reader gets to know and care for (or hate) the people your story is about. You might argue that action enables your reader to 'see' your characters but the action a character performs can be totally at odds with who he/she really is. Your character may be acting against their better judgement, or because they are being forced to do something and the only way to really know what's going on in their heads, what they *feel* is through what they communicate to you by way of their own voice.

"Dialogue should always have something 'real' to say, something that moves your story along, something that imparts information the reader needs to enable them to better engage with your writing; connection to, and involvement with, equal enjoyment of, what they are reading. Dialogue can be used to deepen conflict, expose dishonesty and reveal weaknesses in a direct, immediate way which allows the reader to sense tension, affection, inner turmoil."

There are, of course, lots of tricks of the trade that we can use to embellish dialogue and make our characters more interesting by giving them a more exotic flavour. We now live in a multi-cultural society and it is not unusual to encounter people from different ethnic backgrounds wherever we live – and not everyone speaks with an English/British accent, regional or otherwise. To give a flavour of a character's background we can drop subtle hints into the conversation without belabouring the point.

The most common method is by incorporating foreign words and phrases into the dialogue to a) imply knowledge, or b) show the character is of foreign origin. Needless to say, using them in our narrative without clarification can leave the reader feeling ignorant and irritated, so it is essential that a translation is provided.

In the first instance there is the use of common Latin phrases that have almost become part of the English language, although many will be more familiar with the actual modern translation rather than the original Latin. The following are some of the most popular.

Nil desperandum – literally meaning 'Nothing is to be despaired of' but commonly used as 'Never say die'. Example: 'I knew Reggie was at the end of his tether but his parting words were typical of the man. *"Nil desperandum*, old boy, *nil desperandum."* Never say die.'

Nil carborundum – self-explanatory modern army ranks slang for 'Don't let the bastards grind you down'; the term is now so well known that people believe it to be 'real' Latin.

Caveat emptor – 'Let the buyer beware' is an ancient legal term but it can be used in everyday speech as a warning. Example: *"Caveat emptor,"* muttered Laura with a shake of her head. "He knew you'd feel sorry for that horse and buy it regardless. Now it's going to cost you a fortune at the vet's because you won't send it back to be shot. So stop complaining. First rule of horse trading – let the buyer beware."

Carpe diem – literally meaning 'Seize the day' and used from ancient times until the present to mean 'enjoy yourself' – often interpreted as 'seize the moment' meaning don't miss an opportunity. Example: "You know what they say, Sis, *carpe diem*. Seize the moment! Well, I seized it with a vengeance and despite the initial financial benefit, I'm now detained indefinitely at Her Majesty's pleasure. And I don't regret it for a moment!"

Simon Raven, himself a classics scholar, usedgenerous quotes from the Classics to embellish his *Alms for Oblivion* series, by using Cambridge University characters bouncing quotes and translations off each other to illustrate a point. Since these were learned men, the use of classic Greek and Latin was not out of place in the dialogue, whereas 'pub' Latin can be used by anyone from any walk of life.

When it comes to injecting foreign words to indicate that the speaker is, him or herself, French for example, we can throw in the odd *merci* or *bonjour* because everyone knows this means 'thank you' and 'good day' but anything more adventurous needs clarification. In *The Wild Horseman* the exchange with the French countryman was handled in the following manner...

Engrossed in their preparations, they were suddenly aware of a shadow appearing in the doorway, and instinctively Richard's hand reached for the hunting knife. It was an elderly man, leaning on a bicycle, and it was obvious from his clothes that he was a local farm-worker but there was a challenging gleam in his eye. The walrus moustache bristled. "*Monsieur ... Madame ...*"

"*Bon jour, monsieur*," said Jenny stepping into the courtyard, and wiping her hands on a towel. Deliberately she walked away from the door so their visitor couldn't see inside.

Outside, a rapid conversation was going on that Richard

couldn't follow. His French was always limited to slow, carefully enunciated phrases because *Tante* Isobel had always insisted on speaking English during his visits; in the early years to improve Christian's speech and later for the benefit of her daughter-in-law and the grandchildren. As a result, understanding the gruff *patois* of a localised dialect was out of the question.

He heard Jenny mention '*Alençon*' and stepped outside to warn her not to say any more about their plans. There was still a lot of gesticulating until finally the Frenchman wheeled his bicycle over to where Richard stood and held out his hand.

"*Bon chance, monsieur,*" and mounting his bicycle, he peddled off, calling out something else but Jenny only caught the words *à l'outrance* – 'to the bitter end'.

Similarly, when encountering the German paratrooper whom he'd met before the war started Richard used what little German he knew out of courtesy...

"Ride hard for the coast, *Herr* Hunter. They won't stop ... nothing can stop them."

Those had been the parting words, spoken by the Jewish woman and Richard had a strange sensation of *déjà vu*. "*Danke schön, Herr* von Nehring," he said hesitantly, using the few German words he knew. "*Es guthaben,* be lucky."

By dropping in the odd phrase or colloquialism we enrich the narrative and help to give the foreign element of our story more depth. One of the most colourful for the writer is the use of Yiddish (as opposed to Hebrew) which crops up everywhere and is possibly one of the most expressive of languages. As Fred Kogos explains in *A Dictionary of Yiddish Slang & Idioms*: "Yiddish is spoken by about 10,000,000 people throughout the world. It is widely used in Russia, Poland, Romania, France, England and other European countries. In the United States and Canada, in Israel, South Africa and other African countries and wherever else Eastern European Jews emigrated to, Yiddish survives as a spoken language – in the home, on the streets, in the theatre, in literature, newspapers and the entertainment field."

Anyone with a close working relationship with those employed in industries such as entertainment or the 'rag-trade' quickly absorbs Yiddish into their vocabulary, whilst not necessarily being Jewish themselves. It becomes the jargon and therefore part of our speech patterns where we talk about *schlepping* (dragging) a case around; of something being *kosher* (proper); describe a colleague as a *schlemiel* (an idiot); or congratulate someone by saying *mazeltov*! According to Kogos, there are about 500 Yiddish words that have become part of our everyday language in their original form, and which can be found in *Webster's International Dictionary*.

We must also be aware of the differences in the use of language between the English-speaking Americans and British where the former would ask a chemist for a 'rubber' (condom) while a English person would go to a stationers to purchase a rubber (pencil eraser). It can provide the writer with the opportunity for humour (misunderstanding) in confusing 'pants' with trousers (USA) and underwear (UK) – if we write that a character was 'wearing just his pants' it would mean something completely different to an American or British reader. Or a 'vest' which the British wear next to their skin and the American refer to a waistcoat. In an old Mickey Spillane thriller the suspect was described as wearing a 'red vest' and it wasn't until almost the end of the book that the truth dawned that this referred to a distinctive red waistcoat! For twenty chapters the villain had been running around New York in a scarlet t-shirt in the British reader's mind.

Colloquialisms also add rich colour to written dialogue and can be used to offer a suggestion of regional dialect. For example:

"Is it likely to rain later?" Stephen asked the weather-beaten farmer.

The man narrowed his eyes and gazed into the distance. "Not for another hour or so, but it's a bit black over Bill's mother's."

Stephen's mouth gaped open at this irrelevant piece of information. "Who's Bill?" he finally asked, turning to where the farmer's gaze still lingered. On the distant horizon huge black storm clouds were gathering. *You fool,* he thought to himself, *it's another of those old country sayings that mean absolutely nothing to outsiders.* "Aaah! If my grandmother saw rain clouds over the next village, she knew she had about ten minutes to get the washing in," he offered as an indication that he'd understood what the farmer meant.

This example came from rural Northamptonshire and still causes blank expressions when used out of the area. Older people who have lived in a particular area for all of their lives are an excellent source for such sayings, which can be used to enrich dialogue with a bit of light-hearted banter. The dictionary definition of colloquialism is 'a form of expression used in familiar talk' and regional speech can be enriched by using local words or expressions, although long tracts of dialect should be avoided at all costs since they are incomprehensible and only serve to irritate the reader. Each region has a treasure trove of localised words for things and this gives a far greater indication of background than lines of 'Eee'ers' and 'Eee by gums'.

Each community (anywhere in the world) has its own regional way of speaking and if you are using a setting that is unfamiliar, it may be a good idea to read a few books that give the flavour of the area before using localised characters in your novel or the dialogue will not ring true. Especially if the story is set prior to the 1970s – after which time 'everyone and his wife' seemed to be on the move and technical jargon became the order to the day.

Since that time, Americanisms have become the international currency in language, and we can go to the far reaches of the earth only to find a Thai taxi driver asking: *"Hey Mac, where you from? New York?"* in his best Brooklyn accent. Probably there are more people in the world familiar with the catch-phrases of Clint Eastwood's *Dirty Harry*, than they are with quotes from Shakespeare, courtesy of digital television, DVD and the internet.

When we step into the worlds of science fiction and fantasy, we still need to obey the laws of writing dialogue as Krystina Kellingley explains: "When writing a story set in another world, dialogue can be used very effectively to give your alien characters their 'otherworldly' identity. Just the simply device of dropping the use of contractions in dialogue can make a character sound alien. This is very often used successfully in fantasy fiction, perhaps less so in sci-fi, where dialogue is more often used to introduce strange words (for items we haven't developed yet) or to reference organizations or anomalies in a way of life or belief systems, and of course, to impart knowledge we, in our present time, don't have. Both these settings rely strongly on dialogue, inner or outer, to communicate any apparent disparagement between external action and inner motivation.

Below is an example of dialogue from, *Eladria* by Rory B Mackay, a fantasy epic which illustrates how quickly good dialogue can move a story on. In this short exchange the reader can immediately see that something is wrong. The words chosen also immediately create a world which is obviously not the one we live in: 'It's off course by eighty-six tessits.' And 'Have you contacted the planet surface?'

"We've sent two escort craft to intercept the king's transport. As of yet, there's been no word from either. We've been trying to contact them, but there's been no response."

"Have you contacted the planet surface? You could get one of the military bases to use their scanners and—"

"I've already—"

"Administrator!" interjected one of Jusaad's technicians. "The king's transport has just entered the peripheral zone of short range scanners."

Eladria's heart leapt.

Jusaad joined the technician and leaned over the console to check the readings. "That's the royal transport all right, but it's not on the standard trajectory. It's off course by eighty-six tessits."

"Which means what?" Eladria asked.

"I don't know." Jusaad stood up and rubbed his forehead wearily. He turned to the communications officer. "Officer Nolahn, open communication channels."

The raven-haired communications officer complied. But after a moment she shook her head, a puzzled look upon her face. "We're getting a response, but it's text-only."

"Well, what does it say?"

"According to the message, they've been having problems with their engines, navigational and communications systems. They suspect sabotage. They managed to patch up their engines, but navigation remains affected and the visual communication system is inoperative. They request we initiate arrival procedures."

"That would explain a few things," Eladria said, relieved.

"Perhaps," Jusaad answered with a measure of uncertainty. "But they make no mention of the escort craft I sent to meet them. And I'm not entirely sure I believe this notion of sabotage. If a saboteur had really gained access to that transport, you can guarantee it'd be in a million pieces by now."

Regardless of where we as writers travel in our imagination, we take our language with us because this is the 'tool' we use to tell the story. We cannot invent a different language for our futuristic or other-world adventures as it will be incomprehensible to our readers – although Anglo-Saxon scholar and the greatest fantasy writer of all time, J R R Tolkien created 'elvish' for his *The Lord of the Rings* trilogy.

In *Journey Into Space*, the famous 1950s sci-fi radio series written by Charles Chilton, Lemmy Barnet softly intones a *kaddish* or mourner's prayer for a deceased crewman. Lemmy's character is interesting because it portrayed a working-class Jewish lad from London's East End who was one of the first men in space at a time when such an idea would have been socially preposterous. Chilton's introduction of such a character, together with what must have been recognisable Yiddish humour, proved to be an inspired addition to the rather stuffy and intellectual personalities of the rest of the crew. Chilton later novelised the series that was later released by Pan paperbacks.

Ironically, in the film version of *The Lord of the Rings* (*The Two Towers*) Legolas makes the same gesture in 'elvish' when Pippin and Merry are presumed dead in the aftermath of the battle between the Uruk-hai and the Riders of Rohan, although this does not appear in Tolkien's narrative. There is the barest hint of 'faith' in the gesture in both instances without the need for further comment.

Even if we are walking in the realms of pure fiction it is still necessary to observe the laws of metaphysics and science, the appropriate jargon still needs to be inserted into the narrative. *In House of Strange Gods* a conversation takes place between members of the Charter House and a person they suspect of conjuring up a demon:

"So ... the Ouija board was set up in here," she indicated one of the cell-like rooms off the main body of the cellar. "Was anyone in charge of it? Or was there anyone in the room most of the time?"

"Alison Mayfield. She said she had a message come through for me but it hadn't spelt my name right, so they didn't bother to mention it."

"We'll need to talk to her. What about the mirror?" asked Jack.

"It was the big mirror that's usually hanging on the first floor landing. Bloody great thing in a gilt frame but we thought it looked the part. Draped with black nets and a velvet curtain, you know."

"No, I don't know," snapped Jack, his psychic hackles bristling on the back of his neck. "You haven't got a bloody clue what you might have brought through here, have you? A complete amateur's balls up!"

"Do you normally allow your *staff* to talk to clients like that?" Petersen rounded on Aliona, placing the emphasis on the word 'staff' to indicate what he thought of her colleague.

"Only when they behave like amateur idiots who think they're qualified to set up their own Hell-Fire Club, and then can't cope with the consequences," she responded.

Andreas coloured beet-red to the roots of his hair but refrained from commenting. He'd never mentioned the Hell-Fire connection but this woman has sussed him out and he was uncomfortable. There had been some perverse satisfaction in exposing the fraudulent mediums who'd turned up to dispose of his unwanted 'guest' but he was suddenly aware that these two normal looking people weren't to be trifled with.

As we've learned, poor dialogue is one of the main reasons for a publisher's reader glazing over when reading a first-time novel, where the author has seen fit to include every superfluous utterance of every-day speech. The purpose of dialogue is to move the story along and to give added dimension to the characters through what they say, and often think. *Creating Meaningful Dialogue* will help to get rid of the dross from your typescript and retain the gold in the story. Try these final exercises:

Exercise 1:

Create a passage of dialogue between two people using foreign/localised words or phrases that would fit comfortably with the *secondary* characters in your novel. Now ask yourself...

- Are you sure they are being used in the correct context?
- Would your readers understand what is being said?
- Have you given sufficient clarification?
- Would the use give added depth to your character?

Don't be afraid to experiment with language in order to enrich your writing. And more importantly, don't save all the best lines for your principal players.

Exercise 2:

Even if we are not interested in writing futuristic or fantasy fiction there are often times when we need to add a little bit of 'otherworldly' speculation or thought to add a new dimension to our narrative. Research a local superstition (from anywhere in the world) and relate it in the form of dialogue with the suggestion of a 'native' relating the story.

And don't be afraid to include these stories in your dialogue to illustrate a point.

* * *

Compass Points: Creating Meaningful Dialogue, with Suzanne Ruthven, author of the novels *Whittlewood* and *The Wild Horseman,* together with the literary 'faction': *Charnel House Blues: The Vampyre's Tale,* which she hopes to follow up with a vampire novel when her current work, *House of Strange Gods,* is finished.

The Writer's Book Shelf

The following titles have been mentioned in the text and may have further use for writers who need help in perfecting the technique of writing meaningful dialogue.

The Book of Similes by Robert Baldwin and Ruth Paris (Futura)

The Book of Tells, Peter Collett (Bantam)

A Dictionary of Yiddish Slang & Idioms, Fred Kogos (Citadel)

Foreign Expressions, compiled by B A Phythian (Guild Publishing)

Gestures, Desmond Morris (Granada)

How To Write & Sell Great Short Stories, Linda M James (Compass)

Name Dropping, Philip Gooden (A&C Black)

Nil Desperandum, Eugene Ehrlich (Guild Publishing)

Passionate Plots, Kelly Michelle Lawrence (Compass)

Penguin Dictionary of Historical Slang, Eric Partridge (Penguin)

The Penguin Guide to the Superstition of GB and Ireland, Steve Roud (Penguin)

Peoplewatching, Desmond Morris (Vintage)

**COMPASS
BOOKS**

Compass Books focuses on practical and informative 'how-to' books for writers. Written by experienced authors who also have extensive experience of tutoring at the most popular creative writing workshops, the books offer an insight into the more specialised niches of the publishing game.